I Saved a Winter Just for You

A Theatrical Presentation

The Work of Many Young Writers
Adapted by

TOM ERHARD

Dramatic Publishing Company

Woodstock, Illinois • Australia • New Zealand • South Africa

IMPORTANT BILLING AND CREDIT REQUIREMENTS

All producers of the play *must* give credit to the author of the play in all programs distributed in connection with performances of the play and in all instances in which the title of the play appears for purposes of advertising, publicizing or otherwise exploiting the play and/or a production. The name of the author *must* also appear on a separate line, on which no other name appears, immediately following the title, and *must* appear in size of type not less than fifty percent (50%) the size of the title type. Biographical information on the author, if included in the playbook, may be used in all programs. *In all programs this notice must appear:*

"Produced by special arrangement with
THE DRAMATIC PUBLISHING COMPANY, INC. of Woodstock, Illinois."

For Bruce, Larry and Dan . . .
With Love

I SAVED A WINTER JUST FOR YOU
A Full-Length Play
for Three Men and Five Women

CHARACTERS

BOY ONE . . . . .Poised, dominant, sometimes macho.

BOY TWO . . .Shy, nervous, ill-at-ease socially. The class scholar.

BOY THREE . . . . . The class clown. Underneath his facade is a
gentle, sensitive young man.

GIRL ONE. . . . . .Poised, popular, at times vain.

GIRL TWO . . . . Introverted and shy, with little social grace but
very sensitive.

GIRL THREE. . . . Filled with turmoil and anger. The world has
hurt her.

GIRL FOUR . . . . A total romantic who hides from reality.

GIRL FIVE . . . . The class clown. Also warm and sensitive.

TIME: The present.

PLACE: A stage.

5

We begin with music — live, if possible, and highly contemporary. The CAST comes through the audience, greeting people warmly and carrying armloads of assorted hand props to help with the pantomiming. Not all props need be carried on but enough to create a feel of spontaneous creativity. When they reach the stage, BOY THREE and GIRL FIVE dance with creative comedy to warm up the audience. BOY ONE and GIRL ONE join in but dance with elegance. BOY TWO, GIRL TWO and GIRL FOUR watch shyly from one side. GIRL THREE sits by herself, away from the others. The music stops.

BOY THREE (warmly to the audience). Hi! Glad you could make it.

GIRL FIVE (to BOY THREE). Glad *you* could make it! You got here *six minutes ago*!

BOY THREE. Well, you know . . . stars make an entrance. (The OTHERS hoot and jeer with appropriate ad libs.)

BOY ONE (warmly but seriously). The real stars of this show are a bunch of talented high school students.

GIRL ONE. That's right. Tonight's performance is based on the writings of young people, done in the last few years.

GIRL FIVE. For the Southwest High School Creative Writing Awards at New Mexico State University.

BOY THREE. Do they speak English down there?
GIRL FIVE. Shut up.
BOY THREE. They haven't won a football game since Billy the
  Kid invented the Shotgun Formation.
BOY ONE. Okay, let's get serious.
GIRL FOUR (at the far side of the stage, to GIRL THREE). Are
  you all right? (Slight pause.) You look . . . upset or some-
  thing.
GIRL THREE (after a slight pause). Bill just broke up with me.
  On my way here, tonight.
GIRL FOUR. Gee, you've gone together all year. (Slight pause.)
  Are you okay?
GIRL THREE (getting tough with herself). Don't worry about
  me.
BOY THREE (to GIRL THREE and GIRL FOUR). Come on,
  you guys, pay attention. (To the audience.) So anyway,
  folks, what we're going to do is . . . What we're going to do
  is . . . (He is totally over-melodramatic.) . . . What we're
  going to do is . . .
GIRL FIVE (bumping BOY THREE out of the way with her
  hip). I knew you'd screw it up. (Warmly, to the audience.)
  Our show's going to run about an hour and a half. We won't
  take an intermission.
BOY THREE (with exaggerated gestures). But there are lots of
  places where you can wiggle or make airplanes out of your
  program or pick your nose.
GIRL ONE (stepping forward). Here's how the show is going to
  work. From these writings, we've picked the feelings that mean
  the most to us and then dramatized them.
BOY ONE (joining GIRL ONE). The stories and poems reflect
  how each of us feels about being seventeen.
GIRL ONE. So you'll all get to know us from the selections
  we've chosen.

BOY ONE. And we think that you'll share a lot of these feelings.
BOY THREE. Okay, guys, warm-up time!
GIRL FIVE. We're going to begin with a few poems that show what it's like to try to become a writer.
ALL (gathering at C and loudly singing the vowels several times, each rendition stretching them a bit more). A-e-i-o-u. Aaaa-eeee-iiii-oooo-uuuu. (As they begin the poetry, ALL enunciate each sound with extreme precision.)
GIRL ONE (very dramatically).
   "A" is black.
BOY ONE (dramatically to GIRL ONE).
   The center of your eye . . .
   the pit of a cave . . .
   the space between the stars.
GIRL FIVE (happily).
   "E" is yellow!
BOY TWO (savoring the sounds).
   Not quite the sun . . .
   leaves in late fall,
   the harvest moon.
GIRL THREE (angrily).
   "I" is red!
BOY ONE (lost in thought).
   Eyes after crying . . .
   cheeks in the cold . . .
   the clouds at sunset.
GIRL TWO (softly).
   "O" is white.
GIRL FOUR (very gently).
   The look of snow . . .
   a baby's mouth . . .
   a unicorn's mane.

BOY THREE (very warmly).
  "U" is bright.
ALL (in unison).
  The crackle of an old man's eyes . . .
  the splashing blue of a storm . . .
  the sunlit surface of the ocean.
 (ALL sit at different elevations and in varying positions, busily
pantomiming writing, some happily and easily, some slowly
with frustration.)
GIRL FOUR (at her seat, romantically).
  Poetry is the ballet of the mind,
  Abstract turnings of the soul . . .
  A dance that's positively inclined.
  Its celebration: love of life!
  Poetry is the ballet of the mind,
  Abstract turnings of my soul. ·
GIRL ONE (rising with calm confidence, walking about,
  pantomiming each image).
  I like to hear the sound of my voice,
  The rhythm of my poems, the feel of my legs,
  Shaped smooth and strong.
  I like the golden hair
  On my arms in the summer,
  The dry drops on my skin
  And the steam after a shower,
  The bright gasp-spasm
  Of stepping from the bathroom
  To the cold of the house.
  I like to stare at my face in the mirror,
  Every pore of my face,
  Every thought in my head
  Dizzy and full, poem upon poem, whirling
  In elliptical orbits.

(She spins, her arms gracefully twirling, then sits.)

GIRL THREE (angrily crumpling and throwing her paper).

    You lie on the floor

    molded into

    a blooming flower

    sprayed with *black bugs*.

    My attack on the written world . . .

    (A slight pause.)

    a crumpled paper.

    (She kicks at the paper.)

GIRL FOUR. Is that . . . because of . . . him . . . tonight?

GIRL THREE. What do *you* think? (She turns her back on GIRL FOUR, who makes a sympathetic move.)

GIRL FIVE (nervous about the previous interchange and changing the subject with bubbly enthusiasm and grandiose-but-appropriate finger gestures). "Words," with apologies to Eleanor Wylie's poem, "Pretty Words." I love silly words, words that laugh out loud . . .

BOY THREE (happily joining in). Words that seem to tickle whenever they are used.

GIRL FIVE. Long, bumpy words like hippopotamus.

BOY THREE. I love words, released, discharged and full of life . . .

GIRL FIVE. Like magnetic fields of gravity battling back and forth . . .

BOY THREE. Extended rays of sunlight rocketed down to earth.

GIRL FIVE (exchanging a high-five with BOY THREE). All *right*!

BOY TWO (after a pause, with a lack of security).

    I'm looking for a word

    that I can hold on to

    with an *answer*

    spelled in every letter.

(GIRL TWO nods in strong agreement.)
BOY THREE.
 "Writing:"
Each creaking of my chewed-up pen
brings about a new thought,
that dribbles out of my brain and
plops onto my paper.
(He is disgusted with his writing.)
GIRL FOUR. (As an example of how the poetry in this play may
   be dramatized, CAST MEMBERS away from the action can
   make hoofbeat sounds while GIRL FOUR turns and looks.)
   Inside,
   White mustangs gallop freely about the edges of a frozen
      field that lies deep within me.
   They are shrouded in a fog,
   Yet sometimes I fancy I can hear the clear whinnies of
      those phantoms,
   Those poems that I have never touched.
   And sometimes, when the dull beat of their hooves seems
      to be near,
   I spin around,
   Half hoping to capture – perhaps – a shadow.
   Alas. When I reach for my pen,
   All but the memory of those quivering, white steeds
   Has vanished.
GIRL FIVE (bouncing up and down wildly, clowny and sing-song
   jingly).
   "Blabber Mouth:"
   Flap my jaws,
   My voice caws,
   Fling my tongue
   At everyone.
   Rattle trap,
   No sound gap.

Lips of blubber
Bounce like rubber.
My teeth glisten.
Listen.

GIRL THREE (to BOY THREE, with disgust). I bet *you* wrote that one!

BOY THREE. Not me. But that's what I call *great literature*.

BOY ONE. You would.

GIRL ONE. Listen to this one. Have you ever been afraid of how your teacher would react to your assignment?

GIRL THREE. Yes!

GIRL ONE.

Mrs. Warren asked us to write about how we felt about
   old age.
I thought about collecting on insurance, and Social Security,
Buying three-wheeled bikes and menopause;
High school reunions and flabby upper arms,
And discounts at drugstores
And sitting next to decrepit old men
Smelling of Old Spice.

GIRL THREE (joining in).

But I looked at Mrs. Warren, my English teacher,
And at the pen I held between shaking fingers,
And *I* wrote about
Crocheting shawls, hugging grandchildren, and baking
   cookies.

GIRL ONE (after a pause).

And she'll never know how scared we were
About writing the "right thing!"

GIRL THREE and GIRL ONE. So we could get an "A." (ALL loudly agree.)

BOY TWO. That's exactly how it is, sometimes.

GIRL TWO (to BOY TWO).
> Of all the things I have to say
> The ones left unsaid
> Were the most important.
> Please read
> Between
> My lines
> And hear what I'm *not* saying.
> I have so much that you should hear.
> I need the security of your approval
> To say it.
> You
> Never cared enough to find out
> Who was missing in myself.
> Please listen to my silence
> And
> Give me back my words.

BOY TWO (after a pause, approaching GIRL TWO hesitantly).
Er . . .

GIRL TWO (suddenly very nervous). W-what?

BOY TWO (panicking, turning away, shrugging). Oh . . . nothing.

GIRL FOUR. I'm tired of sad poems that don't work out right.

BOY THREE. Yeah! Give us a happy one!

GIRL TWO.
> I'm tired of sad poems.
> I think it's time
> For a happy poem.
> (ALL cheer.)
> A poem with flowers, mountains, waterfalls . . .

GIRL FOUR (her refrain throughout is sappily romantic).
> And love.

GIRL TWO. Horses, children, a starry summer's eve . . .
GIRL FOUR. And love.
GIRL TWO. Deserted islands, newlyweds, a circus . . .
GIRL FOUR. And love.
GIRL TWO. Bubblegum, little sisters, a puppy . . .
GIRL FOUR. And love.
GIRL TWO (after a definite pause).
    But who can write of so much happiness
    Without becoming . . . ever so sad?
  (She and GIRL FOUR sigh together.)
GIRL FIVE. *This* one's not sad. It's called, would you believe,
  "A Poet's Strife with Indigestion and Other Gastric Compli-
  cations."
BOY THREE. And you guys talk about *my* taste!
GIRL FIVE (acting this out quite broadly).
    I rock back in my chair
    And cower at a blank sheet of paper.
    It snarls and sneers.
    My Bic Fine Point whines
    As I nibble at her cap.
    A summer breeze coaxes my heavy lids shut.
    My Bic Fine Point plummets to the carpet.
    I sleep for a day, or maybe a decade.
    I sleep in one ear and out the other.
    I roll like a stone and gather no moss.
    I sleep in a place where paper is tame
    And reptilian thesaurus write renegade poems.
    I awake and rock back in my chair.
  (Her surprise increases.)
    My paper has been tamed
    By my Bic Fine Point.
  (A pause.)
    And here on my desk

I find this poem!
  (She shrieks in amazement.)
BOY THREE.
  I borrowed a Bic
  from a poet today.
  Bitten into its cap
  Were one thousand thoughts.
BOY ONE (reclining).
  I lie on the prickly grass in the shade,
  Writing poetry.
  A locust is buzzing on a nearby honeysuckle bush.
  The olive tree above me, with its heady pungency
  And shimmering leaves,
  Evokes memories of summer,
  Long-since withered.
  I reflect upon how quickly things change.
  (He rises and speaks with much emphasis.)
  And I realize . . .
  (To GIRL ONE.)
  We will never be exactly this way again.
  (He and GIRL ONE exchange a meaningful look for a beat.)
GIRL ONE (joining BOY ONE downstage and speaking with
  great strength of purpose).
  I am not afraid of black widow spiders,
  Or planets colliding with the earth,
  But of empty rooms and empty houses,
  And doors swinging on squeaky hinges that are
  Rusting from long disuse.
  I am not afraid of mythical monsters
  Or gold-eating, fire-breathing dragons . . .
  But of growing old . . . and being alone . . .
  And not being able to write a poem!

GIRL FOUR. That's right!

GIRL TWO. Agreed.

GIRL THREE (as she, GIRL TWO, GIRL FOUR and GIRL FIVE cluster together). Write a letter in a second or two!

GIRL TWO. Write a word in a minute.

GIRL FIVE. Writing a sentence may take you an hour,

GIRL FOUR. But writing a poem is infinite. (ALL fervently agree.)

BOY TWO (fervently as GIRL ONE becomes the teacher and they interact throughout this poem).

  Mrs. Orwig,

  You tell me to take a part of myself and put it on paper,

  And hand it in.

(A pause.)

    Who are you?

  Sometimes you play music and tell me to dream and then

  Tell you what I see.

    Who are you?

  Mine is paper number thirty-five and you read it at ten-thirty at night

  And you write "very nice" with a brown pen

  And you give it back to me the next day.

  You laugh and love and live during fourth period

  And you say things no one has ever said to me.

    Who are you?

(A pause.)

  And why do I care so much?

(BOY TWO turns away embarrassed. GIRL ONE reaches out behind him, almost touching him, but not quite, with great empathy. There is a brief musical bridge.)

BOY ONE. Okay, gang. (The OTHERS gather.) Day after day, what's *the one* biggest tension that we all have? (A pause.) Well?

BOY TWO (after a pause, nervously looking at GIRL TWO). Getting girls to . . . notice me.

GIRL TWO (embarrased by BOY TWO). Talking to a . . . boy.

BOY THREE. Eating pizza with a soggy crust. (The OTHERS attack him comically until he surrenders.) All right, all right. (He finds it hard to admit.) Finding a girl who . . . won't laugh at me. (He pauses. BOY ONE looks to GIRL THREE.)

GIRL THREE. Dumb guys . . . who treat you like dirt.

GIRL FOUR. Finding a handsome man, somewhere, to fall impetuously in love with me. (There is a long pause and then ALL look at GIRL FIVE.)

GIRL FIVE. I hate to admit. (A pause.) Finding a guy. (After a pause, to BOY ONE.) Come on. You're not exempt.

BOY ONE. Having all my girl friends understand me. (ALL groan at his ego.) So, okay, we hate to admit it, but relationships are *so much* on our minds. Let's look at some of the miseries . . .

GIRL FOUR. And the delights.

BOY ONE. But not in this poem. (BOY THREE and GIRL THREE act the poem out as BOY ONE recites.)
  The wind is ripping,
  leaving a cold, cold bite.
  People are scurrying,
  hurrying through their errands
  to rush indoors.
(A pause.)
  A boy and a girl are walking through the park,
  not hand in hand,
  but against the wind.
(BOY THREE and GIRL THREE lean, holding hats.)
  He stops,
  places his hands on her shoulders,

and she just looks up at him.
(A pause.)
He turns,
walks away.
She stares after him,
silently crying . . .
against the wind.
(GIRL THREE is extremely disturbed as BOY THREE walks
away.)
GIRL THREE (savagely to Boy Three's back as he continues to
walk away).
This was a planned killing,
Wasn't it?
But I'm not dead . . .
Yet.
Your words sting,
Still,
Bees don't kill,
Neither does your tongue.
It flaps like a snake's,
But you have no venom
In your fangs.
Your tongue is forked,
Stabbing at me
Like it would round peas
On a plate
And missing,
Because they roll away
Just like your words.
They fade,
Are flattened
Into a meaningless pattern:

(There is great power in her final line.)
  Just smashed, green words.
(She angrily walks away. BOY ONE sits, tightly flanked by
  GIRLS ONE and TWO, in school. At first, all three interact
  cordially.)
GIRL TWO.
  She is young,
  I am younger.
  She is make-up pretty,
  I am nubby-freckled.
(GIRL ONE primps.)
  She has feathered hair,
  I have frizzy.
  She is smart,
  I am . . . me.
  She is involved in school,
  I am a hermit during and after.
  I hate her.
(GIRLS ONE and TWO glare at each other.)
  And she hates me.
  We have nothing in common
  Except,
  We like the same brown-eyed
  Soft-haired guy who sits in
  The front of the class.
(BOY ONE and GIRL ONE are engrossed in each other.)
  She sits with him.
  I just watch.
(BOY ONE and GIRL ONE go hand-in-hand.)
GIRL FIVE (as happy/clowny BOY THREE pantomimes the
  actions with her).
  Hands
  buried deep

in faded jeans,
I walk beside you
playing
step-on-a-crack
up the street
past shops
and people,
hardly perceiving
your burnt-out
voice.
(BOY THREE mimes non-stop talk.)
flowing
a little too smoothly
like an artificial stream
of chocolate pudding.
Without hate or passion,
or even much emphasis,
I ask you
to
shut up.
(GIRL FIVE turns her back on BOY THREE.)
BOY THREE (sadly looking at Girl Five's retreating back).
In faded jeans of denim flair,
I loved her once.
Satin gown beneath her hair,
a silky embrace flowing
to the crushed-velvet grass.
Too bad our love wasn't
wash-and-wear.
GIRL ONE (sophisticatedly, to BOY ONE, who has all the
GIRLS clustered by him).
You stand so sure; your
blue satin jacket

wards off knavery.
(BOY ONE makes much of his jacket which may or may not be
  imaginary.)
Its silvery snaps,
its shiny insidious finesse
chop at my chilling concrete countenance.
How long will you stand there
to chip away at me?
Oh, sir, I can resist
your stony physique,
your sharp, mysterious eyes.
But, sir, your jacket,
the blue satin jacket
with the silver snaps
and shiny, insidious finesse
just won't leave me
alone.
(She edges the other GIRLS out and fondles the jacket.)
BOY TWO (walking toward GIRL TWO, who sits reading, then
  stopping, hesitating and retreating).
I should have broken the silence
When I saw you there
All alone in the courtyard.
While passing by I should have
Presented to you the greeting of the day,
Or just smiled politely,
But I was afraid of you!
Your beauty scared me.
(A pause.)
What was I to do?
But to walk away silently.
(He walks away. GIRL TWO puts her hand to her mouth in
  dismay as he leaves.)

GIRL FOUR (bending down as GIRL ONE walks back and forth in front of her, different decorations stuck on her shoes with each pass).
>   Every day at the end of third period,
>   I lean over to stuff my books into my worn backpack.
>   Every day as I'm bent down I watch *her* feet walk by.
>   Today her shoes were pink with glitter;
>   The day before they were black with clear plastic heels.
>   Every day her expensive shoes are different.
>   (BOY ONE comes for GIRL ONE.)
>   And every day her feet walk out of class
>   To meet her football-playing boy friend
>   And her cheerleading sisters.
>   (GIRLS TWO, THREE and FIVE join them. She speaks savagely).
>   I kick the dirt and try not to get
>   Too much in my old sneakers.

GIRL TWO. Sometimes the pressures between guys and girls get way out of hand. For example, do you know that more than a million high school girls get pregnant each year, almost all *un*intentionally? And eighty-five percent never come back to school.

GIRL ONE (coldly, to BOY ONE).
>   I met you at Tiffany's party
>   We talked and drank and laughed and drank.
>   You were really nice.
>   You told me your parents were away,
>   So we left for your house.
>   You showed me your room,
>   The Van Halen and Pink Floyd posters on the walls,
>   Your new Hatachi stereo, and your neatly-made bed.
>   I woke wrapped in your arms.
>   Nothing to mask our bodies.

I watched you sleep and thought you cared for *me*.
(A pause.)
But now *that* night is over.
BOY ONE (as he and GIRL ONE stand, staring stonily at each
other but not touching).
I swore I'd never do it;
yet here I lie on cold
white sheets.
Her flesh and mine become one.
(A pause.)
The sheets are still cold.
(He and GIRL ONE stare at each other in dismay.)
GIRL ONE.
Actually, it's a relief
to get away from the fearful
pain in your eyes.
I can't take it any more.
Not the way you gingerly
touch my waist.
(BOY ONE touches her waist.)
Seeking tell-tale evidence
of
love's
labor.
(She and BOY ONE turn away from each other.)
GIRL THREE. And stuff like *that* can lead to *this:*
I hope never to lead the life
of a typical housewife,
stare at the soaps full of plastic people
and instant potato-flake problems,
stay in my bathrobe past noon
with a saggy face and curlers in my hair,

rush to clean, and fix supper by six
when I can listen to his complaints of
tough roast
stringy beans
and flat beer.
GIRL ONE. Or this.
BOY ONE.

He carries around a notebook with a dirt bike on the cover
    and parties after school,
Not letting up until late Sunday night.
He realizes that graduating from high school isn't
Going to be the big deal.

GIRL ONE.

She gets so sick in the morning that going to school
Is often just too hard.
She lies down on the bed to button the pants she
Bought only three months ago, and realizes
How young seventeen really is.

BOY ONE.

There is no talk about a wedding,
A honeymoon,
A house with a white fence.
He started making payments on an old mobile home.

GIRL ONE.

She's quiet and doesn't tell him how much she
Hates aluminum.

GIRL FOUR (shuddering). Ooooo! Bad news.

GIRL FIVE. But thank goodness, not every dating situation turns out that heavy. In fact, some are downright crazy. This is a story called "The Intruder" and we need you. (She beckons to BOY THREE.)

BOY THREE (running up, making amorous advances). To play the romantic lead.

GIRL FIVE. No. A dog.
BOY THREE. A dog? In a boy-girl story? (A pause.) A dog?
GIRL FIVE. Start practicing your bark.
BOY THREE (disconsolately and *very* softly). Woof.
GIRL FIVE. "The Intruder." (GIRL FOUR and BOY ONE stand close together, near the two side-by-side stepladders. They pantomime happy, animated conversation, plus the other actions mentioned as the story progresses.)
BOY TWO (at a far side). It was summer, and afternoon, and I was cruising on over to Jennifer's house. Jennifer's my girl. (He suddenly sees GIRL FOUR and BOY ONE talking and lurches to a stop.) Look at that! (He stares in angry amazement.) That makes my stomach burn! My Jennifer is nudging some jock! If he touches her again, I'll kill him! (He hides behind a chair or a cube.)
GIRL FOUR. I'm glad you're here.
BOY ONE. I'm glad to be here.
GIRL FOUR. It's wonderful.
BOY TWO. Oh, man, am I depressed. From now on, for the rest of my life, I'm only going to listen to depressing songs. (He looks again.) Ohhh! I want to bawl. Come on, tears, start flowing. I want to show the world that I'm *destroyed*.
GIRL FOUR. You look nice.
BOY ONE. Thanks.
BOY TWO. I can't stand it. I've got to get over in those bushes. I've got to *see* what's going on. (He tiptoes to a different part of the stage and hides again.) He's just a . . . terrorist! Stealing her away like that. Well, if Jennifer thinks I'm going to give up without a fight, she's got another think coming.
GIRL FOUR. You're so much bigger and stronger than I remembered.

BOY ONE. I work out in the weight room all the time.

GIRL FOUR. I'm impressed.

BOY TWO. What does she *see* in him? Just because he's got muscles, that's not what counts to a girl. (GIRL ONE feels Boy One's arm muscle.) Or does it? Girls are supposed to like a guy for his character. Can I help it if I grew straight-up-skinny? I know I'm no Mr. Universe or Robert Redford, but what does she expect? And I *never* treated her bad. Not once. Shoot, I bet I've spent a thousand bucks on that woman. Doesn't she appreciate all the things I've done for her?

GIRL FOUR. Are you glad you're here?

BOY ONE. You bet. You look so . . . mature.

GIRL FOUR. Thanks.

BOY TWO. Look at *that*! She's leaning against the fence so her rear end will stick out like the front of a train! Ohhhh! If he stares like that one more time, I'm gonna walk right over there and . . . well, I'll really be mad. (A pause.) I wonder what her dad thinks of that dude? He *likes me*. I can still remember the time I fixed their lawn sprinkler; her dad took me out for pizza. I bet *he'll* never get free pizza.

GIRL FOUR. Are you hungry? Shall we go get a shake?

BOY ONE. I'm having too good a time right here.

GIRL FOUR. Me, too.

BOY TWO (writhing). It's awful in these sticker bushes. (The arms of GIRLS ONE, TWO and THREE become scratching/ grabbing sticker bushes which he tries to evade.) I *gotta* get closer. Let's see . . . I'll run like a midget hunchback across the street behind her wall. (He runs, bent far over.) Hope she didn't see me. Guess I didn't look too cool. Now . . . if I stand up like a human periscope . . . Oh, rats! All I can see is the back of his fat head. And man, look at those shorts she's wearing. I *told* her never to wear those shorts unless I'm with her. I swear I'll kill that creep. What a jerk. And look at his car. What a heap. Who drives a sixty-eight Camaro now-adays? They're so gimmicky. My station wagon's a lot nicer. His car only seats two; what good is a car like that? (He groans as he realizes the intimacy of the two-seater.)

GIRL FOUR. Comfortable?

BOY ONE. Sure.

BOY TWO. What're they talking about? I betcha' they're mak-ing up all kinds of lies about me. I'm gonna assassinate that guy. And look at his hair. Who likes wavy blond hair, anyway? Looks like Shirley Temple's big brother. (GIRL FOUR and BOY ONE whisper.) I've *gotta* know what they're talking about! (He looks around.) I know! I'll hop the fence in their backyard, then shinny up the drain pipe, climb over the pitched roof, grab that big limb, and crawl 'til I'm right over their head! That'll be so sneaky! Okay, here I go, over the back wall. (He leaps over a chair but is confronted by BOY THREE on all fours.)

BOY THREE. Woof! Arf! Arrrrgggghhh! (He attacks BOY TWO.)

BOY TWO. Oh, no! I forgot all about Jennifer's Doberman! Hey, Fang, you always liked me! (BOY THREE bites Boy Two's trousers violently.) Stop it, Fang! I'm your friend. I give you dog biscuits and Coke and pizza and Twinkies.

BOY THREE. Arrrrgggghhh! (He wrestles BOY TWO to the ground, then stands over him, pants enormously and tries to lick him.)

BOY TWO. I'm not dinner! (He pushes BOY THREE away.) If you slobber one more time, I swear next time I give you a Big Mac, I'll leave the onions on! (He finally evades BOY THREE.) Now, to get up on the roof. (He climbs one ladder. Even though he is extremely close to BOY ONE and GIRL FOUR, they, of course, can't "see" him.) I'm no Tarzan, but it's not hard to get onto the roof. (Up a couple of steps, he steps across to the other ladder. *Note: There is no need for dangerous realism or acrobatics here as the audience can imagine him going from roof to tree.*) There! I'm in the big elm tree right above them. (He looks down and sways.) Ohhhh! I didn't realize it'd be this high. Ohhhh. I don't know how I'll *ever* get down from here. (He balances precariously, waving his arms wildly.)

GIRL FOUR. Gee, David, I really had a nice time today.

BOY ONE. Thanks. Me, too, Jennifer. And I really enjoyed picking up your grandmother at the airport.

BOY TWO. It's getting *serious*. *I* never got to pick up her grandmother! She's actually putting her arms around that gorilla! I'm gonna kick that guy right up the . . . Lucky for him I'm stuck here, or he'd be in big trouble. Gee, he's such a loser. Look, he even parts his hair crooked. Awwww . . . They're both acting so mushy. I don't know whether to puke or pee. (He suddenly loses his balance.) Just then the branch snapped, and I fell out of the tree. (He simply hops down with no attempt at realism. In slow-motion, he rolls over in a crazy movement and comes to a stop at the feet of GIRL FOUR and BOY ONE.) I landed smack on top of his awful car, rolled over once, and landed at their feet!

GIRL FOUR. Charlie, what are you doing here?

BOY TWO (with utter nonchalance). Oh, just decided to . . . drop in.

GIRL FOUR (angrily). What were you *doing* up in that tree?

BOY TWO. Ohhhh . . . all the normal things.

GIRL FOUR. You have a lot of nerve, spying!

BOY TWO (leaping to his feet). *Me* have nerve? Who is this guy, anyway? Your new *boyfriend*? Huh? Your *lover*?

GIRL FOUR. Stop snorting. You sound like an asthmatic crocodile. (A slight pause.) Boyfriend? (She laughs loudly.)

This is my cousin David. The one I told you was coming from
Michigan. He just got here.
BOY TWO (still hesitant). Oh. (He looks dubiously at GIRL
    FOUR, who smiles and takes his arm warmly, then hugs him.
    BOY TWO gives a big, relaxed grin.) Oh! Oh! Hi, David. Gee,
    that sure is a nice car you've got there. (ALL laugh and hold
    the pose for a beat.)
GIRL FIVE (coming forward). Hey, that's a cool story.
BOY THREE. How did I do in my dog debut?
GIRL FIVE. Fantastic. You've even got fleas.
BOY THREE. Can I make two attacks next time?
BOY TWO (laughing). No! You really did slobber on my pants.
    (Brief musical bridge.)
GIRL ONE. We laugh about the problems we have with each
    other, but do you realize how difficult it can be, sometimes, to
    get along with our parents?
BOY THREE. Immmm-possible.
GIRL FOUR. It's not that bad. My folks are really super.
BOY THREE. I know. Mine, too, really. (ALL nod and ad lib
    agreement.)
GIRL THREE. Most of us *are* lucky. But you know what's real-
    ly sad? The whole messy business of abuse.
BOY ONE.   I read an article that said every year two million
    wives and one million children are abused, somehow.
GIRL THREE. Those figures would be *three times as high* if
    every case was reported.
BOY ONE. And it can come in such subtle ways. Take, for ex-
    ample, this story.   It's called "Body and Sole."   That's
    s-o-l-e, sole.
GIRL FIVE. What an awful pun. Is it another funny story?
BOY ONE. Are you kidding? Just listen. (The family in this
    story is in a car made of four chairs. Mother and father are in
    front, the two sons in the back.)

BOY TWO (as the older brother). Our car ride to Florida International University's running field is routine, but I'm a nervous thirteen-year-old and I try not to think of the many different tensions to come.

BOY THREE (as the father, quietly overbearing, not screamingly melodramatic). Do you think that *this* time we can *possibly* find a parking space? Last time was unbelievable.

BOY TWO (as the older brother). As we draw near, I see the other athletes warming up for the race. (Various GIRLS pantomime this.) Some were touching their toes with their knees unbent, some walking on their toes, some bouncing up and down on the turf.

BOY ONE (as the little brother). Look! Kids even littler than me!

BOY THREE (as the father). And look at those old fools. They must be in their sixties. They'd be better to do some good, healthy military drill instead of risking heart attacks by racing.

GIRL ONE (as the mother). I think I see a parking space, dear . . . way over there.

BOY THREE (as the father, sarcastically). *Way over there.* It figures.

BOY TWO (as the older brother, to the audience). My dad, Lieutenant Commander Wilson, takes charge of the mission and swerves our seventy-one Volkswagen into the already overcrowded parking lot. As I slide from the rear seat and walk slowly toward the area where the race will start, I survey the crowd of a hundred or more familiar competitors. (To GIRL THREE, as the boy, Joe.) Hi, Joe.

GIRL THREE (as Joe, doing knee pullups). Hi.

BOY TWO (as the older brother). Well, I guess you're gonna win my race again, aren't you?

GIRL THREE (as Joe, shrugging). I'm gonna try.
BOY TWO (as the older brother, with warm friendship). I bet
   you will win. You're the tallest boy in the class. And a great
   runner.
GIRL THREE (as Joe). Thanks.
BOY TWO (as the older brother, to GIRL ONE). Hey, Mom,
   can you give me my entry fee?
GIRL ONE (as the mother). Here you are. (BOY TWO pays
   GIRL FIVE, who is temporarily the race director.)
BOY TWO (as the older brother). The director of the meet, Mr.
   Lawrence, then begins the course walk-through. (He, BOY
   ONE and the other GIRLS meander around the stage for this.)
   I've run it so many times, I could follow the two-mile cross-
   country course with my eyes closed. But I go anyway because
   it helps me keep my mind off *my* race. The meet director finds
   it necessary to use the gray and white megaphone that hangs
   from his wrist as he points out the bright orange cones that
   serve as course markers. (When the walk-through is over, BOY
   TWO begins his own stretching exercises.) The races for the
   younger divisions must finish before I run. My younger
   brother's race draws my attention. Come on, Robbie, come on!
   (BOY ONE runs in very slow motion with one other GIRL.)
   Robbie was back in the pack, but gradually he moves up, and
   now only Doug Shader is ahead of him. Come on, Robbie!
   Robbie puts on a great kick· and wins his race! (ALL cheer.)
   The crowd is thrilled that such a short kid can beat a long-
   legged opponent. (ALL mill around and congratulate BOY
   ONE.) It's almost time for my race now. I sit on the hard-
   packed ground and pull off my sweat pants over the black
   canvas shoes with upturned toes. I can feel stones through the
   beige soles, but the shoes are light and strong.

BOY ONE (as the little brother). Hey, you're still wearing your
   lucky blue and yellow socks.
BOY TWO (as the older brother). Sure.
BOY ONE (as the little brother, nicely). How can they be lucky
   if you never win a race?
BOY TWO (as the older brother). I don't know. They just are.
BOY ONE (as the little brother). The air is dry today, consider-
   ing this is Florida. Running was easier than usual.
BOY TWO (as the older brother). Thanks.
BOY THREE (as the father, approaching and speaking with an
   air of authority). Well, son, listen closely now.
BOY TWO (as the older brother). Yes, sir.
BOY THREE (as the father, far too bossily). What you need to
   do is try harder. Put some effort into it. You can't lag back,
   especially at the start. You're always lagging at the beginning
   of every race. You've got to put your entire mind and spirit
   into winning. You've got to . . .
BOY TWO (as the older brother, turning to the audience as BOY
   THREE drones on unintelligibly). I do listen to Father, but it
   won't matter because I know he'll be disappointed when it's all
   over and I've lost again. Now he's telling me about some idiot
   he used to know who always threw up after every race he
   won . . . just because he tried so hard. (A slight pause.)
   Sometimes I wish I *could* puke. I'd puke right on his new
   shoes.
GIRL FIVE (as the race director). Last call for the twelve and
   thirteen-year-old race! Everybody over here!
BOY TWO (as the older brother). I feel clammy and weak and I
   wish the race were already over. (The other GIRLS cluster
   around BOY TWO and become racers with him.) The gun goes
   off and I'm lost in a forest of pumping legs as the stampede of
   taller athletes surrounds me. A runner in front of me stumbles
   and falls and I must sidestep quickly to avoid tripping over the

tangled mass of arms and legs. (The RUNNERS pantomime this in extremely slow motion without actually moving around the stage. As the race progresses, the cluster will move slowly in what is more a slow-motion ballet than actual jogging, which would look distracting. They make a gradual circle of the stage. Whenever BOY TWO narrates, he steps out of the pack.) At the half-mile, the race has stretched out and I'm in the middle of the twenty-man pack. I begin to move ahead of those who were winded by the opening burst of speed. As I run, I think of my father. "Yes, sir, Lieutenant Commander," I think to myself. I would curse him out loud if I could spare the extra oxygen. Instead, I only run faster even though it begins to feel that someone has plunged a knitting needle several inches into my left abdomen and is slowly shoving it farther and farther into my laboring flesh. (The RUNNERS gradually move on around the stage. BOY TWO enjoys telling this portion.) For about a quarter of a mile now, I am running with a sluggish green canal to my left and a long row of palm trees to my right. The trees are old and cast their shadows toward the canal, and I flash in and out of the sunlight as I run. There are absolutely no parents along this back stretch and I begin to enjoy myself. In fact, I might even forget about the very race itself but for the stitch in my side. (The RUNNERS move on. The FAMILY goes to the finish area and begins to cheer and shout.) I have been passing runners occasionally, and now there are only five in front of me. I hold my position until there is a half mile remaining. (He rejoins the pack.) A slim youth I have never seen tries to overtake me with a burst of speed that will intimidate me into allowing him to pass. He remains a few steps ahead of me for about one hundred yards, but I keep my pace and soon put him behind me. My breath comes hard now. No matter how fast I suck the air in, I need more. It is cool and fresh and it burns my lungs with each deep, gasping breath. Joe, sandy-haired and well-muscled, is the leader, directly in front of me. His hair flops about. I close in on him. As we turn in to the home stretch, he hears my breathing and starts to pull away. (This is pantomimed in slow motion.) There are two hundred yards left, but they seem like miles. (The FAMILY yells and screams.) Desperately, I begin to sprint. My head is whirling and I feel certain that I will fall. I am almost beside him, and only he and I approach the finish line. I can hear every breath he takes. I can see the sweat running down the back of his neck, and I imagine that I can hear his heart beating slowly as if he were at rest. (The FAMILY cheers louder.) Suddenly, as we approach the line, I see my father. His eyes are flashing and for the moment he looks insane. I realize how much I hate him for the pain and nausea I am enduring. I try . . . extra hard . . . we reach the finish . . . but I am three steps behind Joe. (He finishes the race and collapses. The OTHERS, except BOY THREE, cluster around him. He becomes sick to his stomach.)

BOY ONE (as the younger brother). Wow! He's vomiting!

GIRL ONE (as the mother). Get up! Get up! Are you all right?

BOY ONE (as the younger brother). Come on, get up. (GIRL ONE and BOY ONE help BOY TWO up, draping his arms over their shoulders.) Wow, that was some race. I'm impressed.

BOY TWO (as the older brother, still panting). Because I came . . . so close?

BOY ONE (as the younger brother). No. Because you ran hard enough to puke.

BOY TWO (as the older brother). It comes easy . . . to *you*. (BOY ONE and GIRL ONE release him.)

GIRL ONE (as the mother). I'm very proud of you. That was a fine race. (BOY TWO smiles at her. They slowly approach

BOY THREE, standing away from the OTHERS.)

BOY THREE (as the father, harshly). Well?

BOY TWO (as the older brother, defensively). Well, what?

BOY THREE (as the father). When are you going to listen to me? I *told* you how to win. I *told* you when you start, start fast. You can't hang back in the pack. You made the same mistake last week. Follow my instructions, *do you hear*? (BOY TWO suddenly turns his back on BOY THREE in a gesture of defeated humiliation. BOTH hold for a beat.)

GIRL TWO (after a pause, groaning sympathetically). Poor guy.

GIRL FOUR. That was a kind of child abuse, wasn't it?

GIRL TWO. It's certainly harmful pressure. Kids don't need that.

GIRL FOUR. It's still hard to believe how some parents mess up their kids. And yet we hear stories around school. These things *do* happen. For example, here's a story called "Thou Shalt Not." (Her tone with the title is negative. The OTHERS quickly move the four-chair automobile to a different place on the stage.)

BOY ONE. It was Friday night, just another Friday night. I was late as usual. I was supposed to be at Brian's house at seven-thirty, but it was already eight. (He gets in the car.) Tonight we would probably go up to the land. The land is a spot in the foothills outside of town that was cleared to build houses; but after they cleared it, they never built anything, so we would park up there to drink or get high. We'd done this lots of times, so we knew it was safe. (He is cool, driving with one hand.) I pulled into Brian's driveway and gave two quick shots on the horn. (A car horn sounds.) After a minute, Brian appeared at the window, then the front door opened. (BOY THREE waves to BOY ONE.)

BOY THREE. Goodbye, Mom.

GIRL TWO (as the mother). Goodbye. Don't be too late.

BOY THREE. I won't. (He jiggles impatiently while GIRL TWO pantomimes going in and closing the door.)

BOY ONE. Then we went into our usual routine. (BOY THREE pantomimes the following.) As I backed my car out his narrow driveway, he opened the trunk of his car, which was parked smack in the middle of his front yard. He had given up hope of ever getting it to run so he was using it as a refrigerator. He pulled out a bottle of Peppermint Schnapps and his bong wrapped in a white towel. (These props may be imaginary.) Then he cautiously closed the trunk, trying not to make a sound, and trotted over to my car. (He leans over and opens the passenger door.) Hurry up; I've got the heat on. (BOY THREE hops in and fits the schnapps and the bong under the seat, then closes the imaginary door.)

BOY THREE. It's freezin' out there. (He adjusts an imaginary vent to give him warmth.)

BOY ONE (very cool in his driving). Do you have water?

BOY THREE. Yeah. I put it in the bong this afternoon before Mom got home.

BOY ONE. Good. Then we don't have to stop anywhere.

BOY THREE. We could get something to mix with the schnapps.

BOY ONE. I don't think so. I don't feel much like drinking, especially not schnapps. It's like drinking toothpaste. (He drives for a moment.) As we neared the stop sign at the end of the street, we both saw a dark figure standing on the curb. (BOY TWO pantomimes the following.) We kept driving, but when we got closer, the figure lurched *right* off the curb in front of us! (BOYS ONE and THREE pantomime a dashboard-grabbing, sudden stop.) We skidded about five feet, but it seemed like a hundred! Finally we realized we hadn't hit him. He stood motionless, inches from the hood, his head staring down at the ground, not paying the slightest attention!

BOY THREE. Jesus, that was close!

BOY ONE (throwing his door open and leaping out). What the hell is wrong with you? I almost . . . Hey, I know you. You're . . . Ross. Ross Reardon. (BOY TWO does not look up.) Hey, it's me, Michael Couch. What the hell, are you tryin' to get killed or what?

BOY TWO (standing like a frightened rabbit for a long moment). I didn't see you.

BOY ONE. You were lookin' right *at* us!

BOY THREE. Come on, get in the car and let's go. It's cold.

BOY ONE. Wait a minute, Brian. Hey, Ross. You almost ended up a hood ornament. (He begins to get sympathetic.) Hey, where's your coat?

BOY TWO. I don't have it.

BOY THREE. Well, that's real swift. Why doesn't he have it?

BOY TWO (after a moment of silence, his voice shaking). I locked myself out of my house and nobody's home.

BOY ONE. Oh, wow. Really.

BOY THREE (opening his car door and standing with one leg out of the car). How could you do that?

BOY TWO. I just went outside to call my cat and I guess the wind blew the door shut.

BOY ONE. Well, let's not stand in the middle of the street all night. Get in the car and we'll figure something out. (He and BOY THREE get in and shut their doors. BOY THREE reaches back to unlock the rear door. He yanks on the imaginary inner handle simultaneously with BOY TWO, who yanks on the outer handle. The door does not open.)

BOY THREE. Wait a minute! (He and BOY TWO yank on the door simultaneously and the door doesn't budge.) You jerk! *Wait* a minute, willya? (BOY TWO nervously steps back. BOY THREE finally gets the door open and BOY TWO hops in back.)

BOY ONE (driving again). How long have you been out there?

BOY TWO. You talking to me?

BOY ONE. Yes!

BOY TWO. About forty-five minutes.

BOY ONE. You must be cold.

BOY THREE. So where are your parents?

BOY TWO. I don't know.

BOY THREE (twisting around to face BOY TWO). Well, when do you *think* they'll be home?

BOY TWO. I don't know.

BOY THREE. Well, *what*? Ten minutes, an hour, two light years?

BOY TWO. I don't know. (BOY THREE groans in exasperation.)

BOY ONE. Tell ya what. Why don't you come with us and we'll bring you home later? Is that okay? Ross? Because there really isn't much else you *can* do. (BOY TWO nods without enthusiasm.)

BOY THREE. Jeez.

BOY ONE. Let's just head for the land, the way we decided. ·

BOY THREE. Some fun that'll be now.

BOY ONE (to the audience). As I drove, I looked back at Ross in the mirror. He looked the same as last time I saw him. It was in eighth grade. He was always smaller than the other guys, pale and skinny, a sickly kid. Everybody just kinda ignored him. He was content to sit in class and not say a word. (He pantomimes the following from the driver's seat.) I sat next to him in Mrs. Henniken's history class. Whenever we were supposed to be taking notes, he would just sit there and draw pictures. I liked to watch him; he was good. But he always drew weird things: people without arms or legs, or real deformed faces. I remember once he drew a woman nailed upside down on a wooden cross. It was real graphic with globs of blood and a weird look on her face. As he drew it, he giggled to himself. I thought that was really weird, but the picture was the best he'd ever done. I leaned over and whispered, "Hey, that's pretty good," but he panicked, threw the picture into his book, and closed it, folding his skinny arms over it like . . . like a *Playboy* when your mom suddenly walks into your room.

BOY THREE. Hey, daydreamer, wanna stop and get something to drink?

BOY ONE. Yeah, maybe we should get a Coke. Here's a Seven-Eleven. (He turns back to BOY TWO.) You want anything?

BOY TWO. Um. Um. No, thanks.

BOY ONE. Okay, we'll be right out. (He and BOY THREE leave the car and enter a store run by GIRL FIVE.) Yeah, lady, I'll take two Big Gulps. Make one a root beer and one a Coke.

BOY THREE (as GIRL FIVE hunches over the counter, leering at *National Inquirer* and ignoring the BOYS). Hey, lady, you gonna take all night?

GIRL FIVE (finally). Huh?

BOY ONE (disgusted). Two Big Gulps. One root beer and one Coke.

GIRL FIVE (turning slowly to get the drinks). Sure, hon.

BOY THREE (in a stage whisper). Her polyester pants remind me of a sack of mashed potatoes. (In a normal tone.) Oops, I hardly have enough money.

BOY ONE. Maybe we should beat up Ross and take his wallet.

BOY THREE. Boy, *that* wouldn't be hard.

BOY ONE. We couldn't just leave him without a coat.

BOY THREE. I don't even know him that good. The only thing I remember about him is the time I was in the office getting something for Mr. Hamill, and he was in there with his mom 'cuz they wouldn't let him back in class until he got some shots or something. And she was yelling and screaming . . .

GIRL THREE (as the mother in the memory scene, at the far side of the stage). I tell you, Mrs. Principal, the Lord does not want us to be polluted with vicious drugs.

GIRL ONE (as the principal). But we're not talking drugs. These are standard immunizations.

GIRL THREE (as the mother). Handmaidens of the devil. Infiltrating our holy bodies.

GIRL ONE (as the principal). Mrs. Reardon, safeguarding your son from polio is one of the healthiest things we can do.

GIRL THREE (as the mother). The work of darkness. Inspired by Communists in the schools. I will have to cleanse my son.

GIRL ONE (as the principal). But, Mrs. Reardon . . .

GIRL THREE (as the mother). You have polluted him.

BOY THREE (the focus back in the car again). What a bunch of crap. (He and BOY ONE get in the car. BOY TWO has been staring aimlessly out of the window.)

BOY ONE. You sure you didn't want anything?

BOY TWO (tonelessly). Yeah. (They drive, with sharp curves that swerve their bodies sideways, and finally reach the land.)

BOY THREE. I hope nobody's up here.

BOY ONE. It's way too early. (They go over a couple of final bumps which throw the BOYS upward, then finally stop.)

BOY THREE. It's always such a neat view, looking down on the city.

BOY ONE. Yeah. Let's wait a second before we put the heat on. Let me see if I can get the radio to work.

BOY THREE (pantomiming getting his bong from beneath his seat and preparing it). Hey, Ross, do you get high?

BOY TWO (after a long silence). I . . . I don't . . . know. I . . . guess.

BOY THREE. You *guess*! Either you do or you don't.

BOY TWO. I mean I never have, but I'll . . . try it.

BOY ONE. That's good, 'cause that's all we're gonna do for a while.

BOY THREE (banging on the imaginary dashboard radio). Your dumb radio!

GIRL FOUR (from the far side of the stage). Here, now, at seventy-seven on your dial we're doing an album-side weekend. Here's side two of Pink Floyd's *Dark Side of the Moon*. (You may use any current hit. The music plays briefly and then fades down under the dialogue.)

BOY THREE (happily). Ahhhh. (He smokes, then hands the bong to BOY ONE.)

BOY ONE. Now, watch me, Ross. Put your thumb back here and inhale until you see smoke in the chamber, then let your thumb off and inhale fast. (BOY TWO leans forward to observe.)

BOY THREE. But don't take too big a hit 'cause ya'll cough and choke if you do. (He cracks the car window and blows out. BOY ONE hands the bong back to BOY TWO, who inhales too quickly, without expression. BOY THREE takes the bong. BOY TWO sputters into Boy Three's neck and he responds angrily.) Come *on*, Ross!

BOY ONE. That wasn't too bad, was it? Only crack your window and blow outside. (There is a long, content silence.) I don't see you around school.

BOY TWO (after a long pause). No.

BOY ONE. So, how come?

BOY TWO. Ohhh. (Silence.)

BOY ONE. So?

BOY THREE (after a silence). Jeez.

BOY ONE (impatiently). So how come we never see you?

BOY TWO. My mom teaches me at home. (There is silence as the music in the background stops. BOY ONE turns the knob back and forth.)

BOY THREE (giving the radio a hard smack). Shit.

BOY ONE. Well, that's it for the music. The last time this happened, my brother had to take it apart. And the tape player doesn't work, either.

BOY THREE. Terrific. (ALL sit, staring dully at the lights of the city.)

BOY ONE. Now what?

BOY THREE (after a long silence). Oh, man, I almost forgot. I've got a secret to tell.

BOY ONE. What's that?

BOY THREE. But you can't tell anybody.

BOY ONE. You know I won't.

BOY THREE. You, too, Ross.

BOY ONE. Who's *he* gonna tell?

BOY THREE. Okay, you know that pile of dog crap somebody put in Miss Tilley's room? I know who did it. (BOY ONE and BOY THREE laugh uproariously.)

BOY ONE. Who?

BOY THREE. This guy in my English class. His name is Arvester or something.

BOY ONE. He better hope he don't get caught.

BOY THREE. No kidding. (He and BOY ONE laugh. BOY TWO maintains a vacant look.)

BOY ONE. You know what my secret is? Remember those video recorders swiped from the library last week?

BOY THREE. Yeah?

BOY ONE. I know who took 'em. But you *really* can't tell anybody about this.

BOY THREE. I won't.

BOY ONE. Are you sure?

BOY THREE. Yes, I'm sure. (BOY ONE turns around to check BOY TWO, who stares out the window.) All right, who?

BOY ONE. You know Mark Tanner?

BOY THREE. The guy with the sort of greasy mustache and fingerprints on his glasses?

BOY ONE. Yeah. He said he saw them in the back seat of his big brother's car.

BOY THREE. Really? He's over eighteen. He could go to the pen. (Silence.) People do some crazy things. (Silence.)

BOY ONE (finally). Okay, Ross, now it's your turn to tell us a dark secret.

BOY TWO (in a soft voice). Okay.   (BOY ONE and BOY THREE wait in silence.)

BOY THREE (finally). Well?

BOY TWO (very slowly). Tonight . . . before I ran into you guys—

BOY THREE. It was *us* who almost ran into *you*!

BOY TWO (struggling to get each word out). Before I saw you guys . . . before I ran out of my house . . . (A pause.) . . . I . . . killed my mother.

BOY THREE (totally clowny). Well, *that's* nice. (He gives a raucous laugh.) Hey, Mike, didja hear that Nancy's pregnant and her mom threw her outa the house? (He does a comic doubletake to BOY TWO.) So. How'd you kill the old lady? With a wet noodle? (He and BOY ONE laugh uproariously.)

BOY TWO (after a long pause). She was in the kitchen, making bread.

BOY THREE. What's he talking about?

BOY ONE (convulsed with laughter). How he massacred his mom.

BOY THREE (with continued laughter). Oh, that's right.

BOY TWO (quietly). I walked up behind her. I was standing right behind her and she didn't even notice. (He stares out the window as if the other BOYS aren't there.) If I had somebody behind me, I'd notice. But she just kept on making bread, smacking the dough the same way she always smacks me, but she didn't seem to enjoy it as much. I didn't mean to break it; I told her it was an accident, but she just kept on hitting me the way she always did.

BOY ONE. Ross kept on in that low monotone. I looked over after a while and noticed that Brian's head sagged down. He always fell asleep when we sat out here. Ross kept on, and I began missing words, so it's hard to say how long we sat there. Ross kept going on and on about how he didn't mean to break something or other, and how she kept hitting him.

BOY TWO (droning on). So I stood right behind her, waiting for the moment. (A pause.) I raised the knife over my head. I could hardly keep it still. My hand was shaking. I wanted to do it but couldn't. I stood there waiting, then I guess she heard my heart pounding, 'cause she looked up. I saw her reflection in the greasy window pane. She saw me, too, but she just stood there. I wanted to bring the blade down on her head with every bit of strength I had, to hear her skull crack, see her eyes roll back into her head. I wanted it more than anything in my life. (A pause.) Then I realized. (He laughs, for the first time, in a strange, chilling way.) All that I had wanted, all that I had prayed for every second of every day had actually been done. Mother was lying on the ground in front of me. Her stringy white hair was plastered over her face. (He laughs.) I turned off the kitchen lights, and then I ran into the front room where I turned off the lights for her, just like a good boy. (He laughs.)

BOY ONE. Brian! Hey, Brian, wake up!

BOY THREE (thickly). W-what?

BOY ONE. Ross is freaking out from the dope. (BOY THREE turns to look at BOY TWO, who sobs, his face buried in his hands.)

BOY THREE. What happened?

BOY ONE. *He killed his mother*!

BOY THREE (laughing). Bull shit. (BOY TWO sobs louder.)

BOY ONE. I'm serious. He's been talkin' about it for about an hour. Then he started freakin' out.

BOY THREE. Hey, Ross! (BOY TWO emits more sobs.) Well, what the hell. What do we *do*?

BOY ONE. I don't know, but I don't think he's messin' around.

BOY THREE. You think he *really* killed his mom?

BOY ONE. I don't know. I mean I *don't know*!

BOY THREE. Well, I don't want to stay here, with *him*.

BOY ONE. Neither do I, but where do we go?

BOY THREE. Let's take him home.

BOY ONE. He said nobody's home.

BOY THREE. Well, let's check it out, anyway. (BOY ONE starts the car.) What about the creep's dad?

BOY ONE. They're divorced. I remember that one of 'em tried to shoot the other one outside of church one Sunday.

BOY THREE (turning back to BOY TWO). Hey, Ross. Ross! Hey, man, are you okay? (BOY TWO continues to sob. BOY ONE drives rapidly. All three BOYS careen from side to side. To BOY ONE.) How long was I asleep?

BOY ONE. I don't know. Maybe an hour.

BOY THREE. What was he sayin'?

BOY ONE. I hardly even heard. Something about chopping her up. And pools of blood.

BOY THREE. Maybe he's just spaced out.

BOY ONE. I hope so. I always wondered what was going on, inside his head. All those weird drawings. I mean, they were strange. I always thought he was weird, but never *really* weird.

BOY THREE (pointing). This next left. (BOY ONE turns sharply and brakes.)

BOY ONE. No. Other end. What are we gonna do when we get there?

BOY THREE. Just drop him off and peel rubber.

BOY ONE. But what about his mother?

BOY THREE. I don't know. What about it?

BOY ONE. You didn't hear him. The way he was talking. Brian, I think he really did it.

BOY THREE. Well, let's just dump him at his house. (He turns around as BOY ONE jackrabbits into a start. ALL jolt and sway.) Ross, can you hear me? (There is no response.) Look, we're almost at your house, okay? We're takin' you home, and we'll see if we can find a way to get you inside. (He turns back to BOY ONE.) I don't know *what* his problem is!

BOY ONE. Hey! (BOY TWO pantomimes jerking the back door of the car open and jumping out while the car is still in motion. He rolls over and over on the street.) Jesus! (BOY ONE jams on the brakes and brings the car to a stop. He and BOY THREE run to BOY TWO, on the ground. Boy Two's arm is bent awkwardly. BOY ONE and BOY THREE approach slowly.) Ohhhh! He's all messed up!

BOY THREE (hysterically). What do we do?

BOY ONE. Have to get help!

BOY THREE. Shit! We never should have brought him along!

BOY ONE. Never mind that. Wait here. I'll go to the first house with a light on.

BOY THREE. Okay. Hurry. (BOY ONE starts off.)

GIRL THREE (as the mother, screaming viciously from the opposite direction as BOY ONE turns and begins toward her, then stops). Ross! Ross! Where are you? We know you can hear us. If you don't come back inside this minute, Ross, we're going to have to punish you for the second time tonight. Punish you, Ross. (A pause, then she speaks slowly.) The Lord and I will have to punish you.

GIRL ONE (after a suitable pause for the story to sink in). If you think that story was scary, listen to this poem. It's called

"My *Beloved* Father:"
You fertilized me with your so-called love.
Now I have grown from your deadly stigma
Into a woman in a child's body.
You whisper in my ear and taunt me with your desires:
The take-and-give game is what you call it.
I am immobilized to your touch, as you caress my body.
Deep inside you, I reach and touch your love,
Which is buried under your wicked thoughts.
I rest in your evil arms:
Blindly I am your child.
You hold me and caress my tender skull,
Then grab hold of my neck,
Licking, stroking with your speared tongue,
(A pause.)
Until you leave me . . . alone . . . and naked.
(There is silence and then ALL emit low murmurs.)

BOY ONE. Wow! (A pause.) You know, abuse can come in a lot of different ways. Sometimes, it's all tied up with our childhood loss of innocence about older people. Take, for example, this story. It's called "The Haunting Voice of My Laughin' Pa." (GIRL ONE serves as the narrator. BOY THREE, who does *not* play for comedy here, is the boy. The cats are imaginary, as is everything else in the barn. The stepladders are the loft. Whenever GIRL ONE narrates, BOY THREE pantomimes to fit the actions described.)

GIRL ONE (narrating as BOY THREE leans across a ladder top). As nine-year-old Abe looked up at the brown beams that supported the barn's roof, he noticed the spider web. The sun's rays slid through the holes in the roof and made the web's design sparkle. The heat was sticky and the smell of manure lay heavy in the barn, even in the hayloft.

BOY THREE. That straw dust itches. It's stickin' to my bare feet like burrs on socks.

GIRL ONE. Wiping his sweaty neck with his grimy hands, Abe turned on his stomach to get in a more comfortable position on the straw.

BOY THREE. Boy, if this ain't the life.

GIRL ONE. Abe closed his eyes and was glad to be away from the house, away from work, and alone with Billy, his cat.

BOY THREE. This is nice. A world all my own. A place to think, Pa always says . . .

BOY ONE (at the opposite side of the stage, not in the action but obviously a voice in Boy Three's mind). Only a lazy man thinks.

BOY THREE. I know Pa's mistaken. I jes' know he's gotta be.

GIRL ONE. Getting on his knees, Abe laid his face against the cracks in the hot wood and peered out of the barn to see if his pa was around.

BOY ONE (as the memory voice). I want you doin' chores. No settin' around.

GIRL ONE. Turning around, he decided to go and check on Billy. Named after Billy the Kid.

BOY THREE. Billy, I swear, day after day I've been bringin' milk up here to ya, and ya jes' gettin' more and more sickly every day. Yer jes' layin' around and gettin' all bloated. Jes' as if you'd eaten a lot of green apples. But, Billy, I don't think you'd ever eat *any* color of apple.

GIRL ONE. Abe crawled over to the corner, to Billy the Kid. As he stroked Billy's golden head, the cat began to purr.

BOY THREE. I sure like you, Billy.

GIRL ONE. As he lay there on his stomach petting Billy, for some reason Abe started thinking about death.

BOY THREE. You know, Billy, it don't scare me none at all.

'Cause I know I'm goin' to heaven. Hell ain't for me. I jes'
don't like the heat. It's even too hot right here. But Pa's
the one has to worry. Now *he's* goin' to hell! He's goin' for
sure, 'cause he never has given Mama nuthin'. And he jes'
works us all the time . . . even little Ralphie, and he's only
three! If Pa ever dies, I'll be the head of the family. I'd be
better to the kids. (He sighs.) Mama's gonna have still
another baby. Seems like she's always havin' 'em.

GIRL ONE. Billy the Kid gingerly moved positions and began
to meow again. Abe got off the bales.

BOY THREE. Okay, okay, I'll get you some more milk. I know
you're not *too* sick.

GIRL ONE. He climbed down the ladder, grabbed a bucket and
began milking Bessie. When there was milk covering the bottom of the bucket, he started back to the loft.

BOY THREE. Boy, I'm sure gettin' used to climbin' with two
feet and one hand. Gotta hurry, gotta hurry.

GIRL ONE. In his excitement, he dropped the bucket. The
warm, white milk poured out over the dry, brown manure on
the barn floor.

BOY THREE. Well, let's try again. (He milks the imaginary cow,
then climbs back up.)

GIRL ONE. As he climbed, a giant splinter rammed between his
first and second toes.

BOY THREE. Owwwweeee!

GIRL ONE. He gritted his teeth, hard, so he wouldn't cry.

BOY THREE. Pa always says . . .

BOY ONE (as the memory voice, still at the far side of the
stage). Only snivelin' old women cry.

BOY THREE. Boy, I sure feel like cryin', but I've gotta get this
milk to Billy. Here I am, old Billy the Kid. I'm back. Gee, I'm
glad you're not cryin' anymore. But golleee, I wish I was like
you and could cry any time I wanted. If I was a cat like you,

I could cry 'til the hurt went away. (He is totally astonished.) Billy! Billy the Kid! You're havin' babies! Lookit here, there's two already. That's right, Billy, lick that slimy junk off. Lookit, one's calico and you're black. Billy, you're not supposed to be havin' babies!

GIRL ONE. Abe sat there, dazed. Soon there were two others. The third was black and the fourth was gold. Billy the Kid licked them clean, then stopped and looked softly into Abe's eyes.

BOY THREE (with loving warmth). Would you like some milk now?

GIRL ONE. Cupping his hand, he poured milk into it and put it to Billy's mouth. Her pink, raspy tongue lapped the fresh, white and warm milk.

BOY THREE. That's it, Billy. Lay your head down. That's right; go to sleep. And look how thirsty those little babies are.

GIRL ONE. As Abe wiped his sticky hands on his dirty jeans, he could see that the kittens were happy.

BOY THREE. My baby brother looks jes' that way when Mama rocks him. Boy, if Pa ever knew about you guys, I'd really get a lickin'. Maybe I better go do some work, so he'll let me keep all of you. I'll go down and clean the barn floor. But first I better pet you, Billy. Gee, your fur is soft. Softer than the feathers under a chicken's wings. (BOY ONE quietly moves "into the barn.") Gee, I love to pet you, Billy. Even if you are a girl.

BOY ONE. Abe!

BOY THREE. Uh, oh! It's Pa!

BOY ONE (looking around). Abe. Abe! Where in thunder are you?

BOY THREE (after a pause, terrified). Er . . . ah . . . up here, Pa.

BOY ONE. What in the hell are you lollin' up there? I told you to *work*.

BOY THREE. Ain't doin' nothin', Pa.

BOY ONE (climbing the second ladder). Liar! (He grabs Boy Three's arm fiercely and shakes him, then suddenly spots the kittens.) Where did *they* come from? (BOY THREE tries to respond, but can't. BOY ONE slaps Boy Three's arm, hard.) Drown 'em.

BOY THREE (with great urgency). I ain't gonna, Pa! I can't.

BOY ONE. Drown 'em, Abe, or I'll beat their heads against the barn 'til they split.

BOY THREE. No, you ain't!

BOY ONE. Yes, I will.

BOY THREE. I love 'em! And I hate you. You're goin' to hell, Pa. You're gonna go to hell.

BOY ONE (laughing). You gonna do it, Abe?

BOY THREE (scrambling to protect Billy and the kittens). No! (He and BOY ONE face each other, across the ladders, motionless.) No! No! (Suddenly, BOY ONE scoops up the imaginary litter of kittens and, one-handed, rushes down the ladder. BOY THREE follows.) No, Pa, no! Ohh! God help me! Don't let him kill those little babies!

GIRL ONE. Billy ran down the ladder after his pa, grabbing Pa's smelly, brown-checkered shirt, trying to get him to drop the kittens. Abe kicked and screamed, but his Pa suddenly swerved and pushed Abe in the face. Abe staggered back. Pa dropped all the kittens except the little black one, which he grabbed hard by the tail and began smashing against the floor boards. Blood spurted out and covered his fingers.

BOY THREE (in hysterical grief). Stop it, Pa, stop it!

GIRL ONE. But Pa gathered up the rest of the kittens with one hand and with the other hung onto Abe's shoulder and marched him out of the barn.

BOY ONE. Fill the bucket.

GIRL ONE.   Abe snatched the three living kittens from his father's arm and set them down on the cool grass. A clump of purple clover loomed up beside them.

BOY ONE. Pump! (BOY THREE pumps, still crying and wiping his tears from his face with his free hand.) Now.

GIRL ONE. Pa stuck his fingers, all bloody, onto Abe's face and smeared them on his right cheek. Abe's body shook and he vomited onto his father.

BOY THREE. I'm glad! (He picks up the kittens, kisses them and cradles them.)

BOY ONE (after a long pause). Now.

GIRL ONE (very slowly). As the tears fell from Abe's face and made ripples in the bucket, his father bent low over him. Abe's eyes couldn't move from the bucket. In back of him, he could see the long dark shadow and could hear the haunting voice of his laughing pa. (A long pause with a brief musical bridge.)

GIRL TWO. That last story was sad. (She sighs.) Thank goodness people are becoming more sensitive about animals these days.

BOY TWO. Do you think they are?

GIRL ONE. I do. I think most pets have a better life than they used to.

GIRL TWO. I hope so.

GIRL FOUR. Except on cold winter mornings. (She chuckles.)

GIRL TWO. What does *that* mean?

GIRL FOUR (giggling). Let me tell you about my cat. (She lies down luxuriously.)

    From under heavy blankets
    I hear my cat outside the window.
    I know I should let her in.
    I know it's cold and snowy
    She's a nice cat,

A tabby.
I had a black cat once
With big green eyes,
A witch's cat.
What was I that Halloween?
Ah, yes, a princess
With white slippers,
White as snow.
Snow . . .
I should let my cat in . . .
The blankets are so warm and heavy,
So warm . . .
(She drops back to sleep with a smile. BOY THREE emits a sad
meow.)
BOY TWO. Aren't cats mysterious? (BOY THREE pantomimes
the cat.)
Cats with hungry eyes
Want the food I take,
But run.
I have come too close.
(BOY THREE scampers off.)
GIRL ONE (using ten fingers as birds, then one forefinger as a
tail).
Soft gray flutterings,
Sparrows on my windowsill . . .
My cat's tail lashes.
BOY ONE (as BOY THREE perches above him on a stepladder).
Heartless,
Ominous, black
Crouching presence high in
Branches above, ready to pounce on
Movements.

GIRL FIVE (delightedly imitating a cat).
    My cat is crouched down
    on the dusty brick
    in the shadow of the potted plumbago vine.
    She is thinking of tigers
    and her tail remembers them,
    and moves over the bricks
    over the bricks
    over the bricks.
    She has spied me watching her
    and her whiskers vibrate with excitement.
    She stands and smells carefully
    the potted plumbago
    and scratches her teeth on the edge,
    as she watches me.
    Then she walks quickly across the brick floor.
    Delicate plumbago blossoms
    Cling by their sticky sap
    to her back,
    like the little bees that follow the lioness.
    With two gleesome leaps she climbs
    into the tree
    and perches on a branch, looking
    down at me.
    She crinkles her skin, from her tail
    up to her shoulders,
    and her ears look down her back.
    The plumbago blossoms tickle her,
    and I *know* what she is thinking.
  (A pause. She giggles.)
    If I were *smaller* than she . . .
    and even wiggled my nose!
  (ALL laugh.)

GIRL TWO (seriously). Here's a story about a dog. I just can't get it out of my mind. It's called "The Stray." (BOY ONE pantomimes as she narrates.) The fourteen-year-old boy walked outside to his bundle of newspapers. It was early morning and the sun was just rising over the mountains. He folded the papers, fit them into his basket and rode off on his bicycle. (BOY ONE sits astride a folding chair as the bicycle. He pedals and looks with his head, but remains motionless on the stage.) About a block from home, a small dog came running out to meet him.

BOY ONE. Hello, there! I've never seen you before. You're a fast dog! I think I'll call you Whippet. (He gets off the bicycle and rubs the imaginary dog with warm affection, then gets back on the bicycle.) Whippet, you gonna come with me this morning?

GIRL TWO. Mike started up again, the dog close behind. (BOY ONE throws imaginary papers.)

BOY ONE. Gee, Whippet, the route went fast this morning. Maybe because of you. We've even got time to stop at the Seven-Eleven for a comic book and a pint of a milk.

GIRL TWO. He rode across Main Street to the store, parked his bike, and opened the door.

BOY ONE. Be out in a sec, Mr. Whippet.

GIRL TWO. The stray dog lay down. The door jingled as Mike closed it behind him.

BOY THREE (as the storekeeper). Hi, Mike. Gonna play some pinball this morning?

BOY ONE. Naw. I don't have enough money. I'll just take a look at your comics for a minute. (He reads the comics.) Wow! "Legion of Superheroes." "The Avengers." "Marvel Two-in-One." Gee. Guess I'll take these three and a pint of milk.

BOY THREE (as the storekeeper). That'll be a dollar forty-eight. (BOY ONE pays him.)

BOY ONE. See ya, Mr. Wilson.

BOY THREE (as the storekeeper). 'Bye, Mike.

GIRL TWO. The boy opened the milk, took one sip, then poured some on the sidewalk. The dog lapped it up happily and quickly. Mike guzzled down the rest, then jumped on his bike.

BOY ONE (pedaling hard). Come on, Whippet! C'mon, dog, let's move. (He looks back over his shoulder.) Hey, idiot! You coming? (In sudden panic, he gives a loud scream.) *No! Wait!*

GIRL TWO. The dog didn't stop. Neither did the car. (A long pause.) The dog lay there in the road. The lady in the Mercedes got out of her car.

GIRL ONE (as the driver). I'm sorry. (She is nervous.) I didn't see him. The sun's so glary.

BOY ONE. Awww, it's okay. It's not my dog, anyway. (GIRL ONE goes off.)

GIRL TWO. Mike carried the dog's body off the road. He set him down gently and softly stroked his head.

BOY ONE. Goodbye, Whippet.

GIRL TWO. Then he mounted his bike and, head down, sped off home.

GIRL FIVE (as the mother, greeting BOY ONE). Mike, I'm going to the grocery store. Want to come?

BOY ONE (getting off the bicycle and into a two-chair car). I guess. Okay, Mom.

GIRL TWO. The two of them took off. The boy's mother began to talk, but Mike paid little attention. Main Street loomed up quickly and the horror flooded over Mike. He buckled his seat belt, held on tight, and closed his eyes.

GIRL FIVE (as the mother). Mike? Mike? Have you been listening to anything I've said?

BOY ONE (opening his eyes). Huh? Oh, yeah. Sure.

GIRL FIVE (as the mother). Is something wrong, Mike?

BOY ONE. Just a small problem. But one I'd rather not talk
  about.
GIRL FIVE (as the mother). All right, but if you want to talk
  about it later, we can.
BOY ONE (as he and GIRL FIVE get out of the car). Thanks.
GIRL TWO. Next morning, Mike walked out to his bundle of
  papers. He broke the plastic strip holding them, folded and
  counted them, packed them onto his bike, and rode off. As
  he progressed around his route, he came upon an old man
  who was looking for something.
BOY TWO (as the old man). Sparky! Hey, Sparky! (He whistles
  hard.) Sparky!
BOY ONE (riding by). Hi, there.
BOY TWO (as the old man). Hi, sonny. Have you seen a small
  dog?
BOY ONE (hesitating a moment). Er . . .
BOY TWO (as the old man). Been gone since yesterday morning.
BOY ONE. Er . . . no.
BOY TWO (as the old man). Sparky! Oh, Sparky!
GIRL TWO. Mike drummed on the handlebars, then rode on.
  The route seemed endless. When he finally got home, he went
  to the phone above the chest freezer in the kitchen and went
  down the list of most-used numbers on the wall.
BOY ONE. Mr. Young . . . The Tribune . . . five, five, five,
  four, two, six, one. (He dials.) Mr. Young? This is Mike
  Downs. (A pause.) Yeah. No. No problems. (A pause.) But I
  am quitting my paper route. Today. (A pause.) Personal
  reasons. (A pause.) That's all . . . personal reasons! Yes,
  thank you. 'Bye.
GIRL TWO. Slowly he hung up the phone and, finally, the tears
  came. (A long pause.)
GIRL THREE. You think that's bad? Listen to this. It happened when I was a little girl.

As I sit in my mud puddle
making my famous pies,
the cat stretches near my feet.
Looking at him,
I recall us by the fireplace
playing the 'get the foot' game.
It happens so fast!
The truck, the cat's dash, the horror.
Stunned people
look at me, with sad eyes.
The guys mowing lawns,
all the children laughing,
all stop.
(She speaks bitterly.)
The driver didn't.
He just kept on going.
(There is a long pause, then a brief musical bridge.)
BOY THREE. Oh, man, I'm hungry.
GIRL FIVE. What does *that* have to do with anything?
BOY THREE. Plenty. We're not taking an intermission, right?
GIRL FIVE. Right.
BOY THREE. So . . . nobody gets a chance to munch popcorn
  or get a Coke. Including me.
GIRL FIVE. So?
BOY THREE (building the suspense). So . . . what's the next
  best thing? We take a refreshment break. *But* . . . you can
  only feed your imaginations! (ALL ad lib such remarks as
  "What's going on? Huh?") We'll do our favorite poems about
  food. (ALL ad lib shouts of agreement such as "I've got one!
  Me first! No, me! Yeah!" as they mill about for a few
  moments. BOY THREE uses wild hand and mouth gestures.)
  Glorious, glorious pizza pie;

Did someone send you from the sky?
I know you were not made on earth,
Too perfect for mere mortal birth.
The wonderful taste I've come to know
Of golden, chewy pizza dough,
Of bubbling piles of melted cheese,
And dark red sauce that's sure to please.
At the pizza altar I kneel and pray,
That you will visit me today.
And then you're here, my saving grace,
So I proceed to stuff my face.

GIRL FIVE (very slowly). I've got a quiet little poem about
food:
In the warmth
of Thanksgiving
and heat
of the oven
there are . . .
(She pauses, then speaks deliciously, with quiet emphasis.)
cranberries.

GIRL FOUR. Poems about food can be romantic, too.

BOY THREE. Oh, you and your romance.

GIRL FOUR. I'm not talking kissy-face. (She uses appropriate
hand gestures throughout.)
The ice cream melts through her fingers.
It feels deliciously cold running down her hand,
to drop off a grubby elbow.
Her feet bare in the dust, but they don't feel
the hot cement like her bottom does, through
dirty blue shorts.
Her summer is forever, and school and snow
will be enjoyed in their own time.
(A pause.)

But now there is ice cream in her fingers,
and the sun is lazy-hot.

BOY ONE.   And here's one called "The Candy Store." (He recites with all the "deliciousness" possible, relishing each sound.)

The sun was high, in purple clouds,
A lemon drop in cotton candy.
The trees were red with crackled leaves,
Licorice with raspberry chips.
The wind was cool, peppermint patty.
The mountains high, a mound of chocolate.
Tall grass green, lime suckers waiting.
The sun goes down. A lemon drop is eaten.

ALL. Yeah! Yeah! That makes me hungry! Great!

GIRL THREE. You guys think all food poems are yum-yummy. Listen to *this* one; it's called "Cafeteria Green Peas." (She walks through an imaginary serving line of the OTHERS.)

And I remember the plastic plates
with metal spoons,
wrapped in cardboard napkins.
And I remember the hard green peas,
stuck on top of my peaches,
next to my Grade A warm milk.
And I remember the skin of my chicken,
with goose bumps full of hairs.
And I remember where it all went:
inside two big silver bins.
There went my chicken, peaches, and peas.
(A pause.)
And I remember that I was *hungry*.

BOY TWO. How about imagining an entire village of wonderful things to eat? Delectable tidbits of scrumptious pineapple float lazily down the lemonade flume.

GIRL FIVE. Mmmm, nice.

BOY TWO. Come on, you guys, let's do this one together. (ALL form a semicircle, each trying to outdo the previous speaker.) Delectable tidbits of scrumptious pineapple float lazily down the lemonade flume.

GIRL FIVE. Banana people toil laboriously in the wishing-well mill.

BOY ONE. Gingerbread houses line cellophane sidewalks, with marshmallow flowers growing in the chocolate soil.

GIRL TWO. Cheese-flavored cats and apple-spice dogs run playfully about mustard-smeared fields.

GIRL THREE. Submarine buses swoop macaroon children to the crackerbox school at the end of the lane.

BOY THREE. The tangerine sun rises ever so sweetly, oozing over the meringue-covered peaks.

GIRL FOUR. High above, cotton candy clouds stick to invisible winds, leaving flocks of orange-flecked birds in their wake.

GIRL FIVE. Bread-dough people whisper of strawberry tales in their discreet little polyethylene hideaways.

BOY TWO. Butterscotch goblins wave their goodbyes as their mineral-laden vessel departs.

GIRL ONE. The honey-rayed fog blends with the horizon.

BOY TWO. And up pops the crisply glowing peppermint drop, to keep night watch over the imaginary village called . . .

ALL. Foood! (ALL laugh.)

GIRL TWO (after a slight pause). I hate to spoil everybody's mood, but do you know poems about food can *really* be about our love lives?

BOY THREE. Come *on*.

GIRL TWO. I mean it. Listen to this. It's called "French Fries." (BOY ONE sits across from her but quickly leaves.)
   When you were gone, I felt like a table
   That is left to be cleared,
   With wadded-up napkins,
   Ice melting in the glasses,
   And greasy french fries lying
   Embarrassed on the plate.

GIRL THREE. That's right. Here's another one. (She pantomimes with her hands and changes mood totally between stanzas, from love to hate. In Stanza One, BOY ONE stands facing her, close and amorous.)
   I peeled the peach
   with perfection,
   leaving not a trace
   of skin
   on the soft amber flesh.
   It wasn't bruised . . . or even tainted.
(Suddenly, BOY ONE spins away from her and snuggles up to GIRL FOUR.)
   With a slow, violent surge
   I crushed it, and I squeezed
   until the
   pit
   cut through my flesh
   and my blood soured
   the sweet, sweet juice.

GIRL ONE. Yes, but there are good moments, too. This one's called "Baskin Robbins." (She recites with light, loving nostalgia as BOY ONE closes in with macho come-hitherness.)
   Vanilla, chocolate, strawberry days
   until
   a honey-haired boy

with seas and skies and
dungarees in his eyes
stomped on my cash register,
scattering quarters and housewives,
and instead of a milkshake . . .
(A pause.)
ordered me.
BOY ONE.   And another one called "Lunch."   (GIRL FOUR
sits opposite him and they stare at each other.)
Sitting inside Jack-in-the-Box
at the brown and orange table,
sunlight coming through the window,
french fries laying in a heap on the red tray.
I sit here looking into your blue eyes
holding onto a cold cup of Coke.
Looking outside and seeing
the different colored cars parked in a row.
Conscious of the feelings of happiness, pleasure,
contentment.
(A pause.)
I'm satisfied.
(A pause.)
I bought
your lunch today.
(He and GIRL FOUR lean across and hold hands. There is a
brief musical bridge.)
GIRL FIVE.   Hey, we should have done the whole show about
food.
BOY THREE. You bet.
GIRL THREE. No way. We can't horse around forever.
BOY THREE. Why not?
GIRL THREE. Because of all that . . . stuff, out there. Look
what's going on: terrorism, revolutions, wars.
BOY ONE. That's right. We don't even know if we're going to

live long enough to have families of our own.

GIRL TWO. Yeah. Some crazy dictator could blow us all up.

GIRL FIVE. I *know* all that. But who wants to think about it?

GIRL THREE. We have to. So we don't make the same mistakes.

GIRL FOUR. My dad was in World War Two and he sure has some awful memories about the D-Day Landing.

BOY TWO. Mine, too. In North Africa. He says we mustn't forget the terrible things.

GIRL THREE. Exactly. And to make us remember, through the eyes of a teenager today, here's a story called "Deja Vu at Dachau." (The CAST MEMBERS make chairs and cubes into a bus at one side. One low cube in front is the driver's seat, with several rows elevated behind him. GIRL THREE sits next to BOY ONE. She begins by speaking to the audience.) As I looked up at the water-stained ceiling of the old bus, my mind began to wander strangely. (She stares vacantly, then speaks more to BOY ONE than to the audience.) Where are we?

BOY ONE. What?

GIRL THREE. Oh, nothing. I suddenly had this weird feeling.

BOY ONE. What of?

GIRL THREE. It's silly. Really. For a minute, I couldn't remember who I was . . . or where I was.

BOY ONE (teasing GIRL THREE). You're Sharon Zelany. You're on an old bus, on a European tour with an American teenage choral group. And last night we performed in Ulm, West Germany. Does that help?

GIRL THREE (in a nice way). Don't make fun of me. It was . . . I don't know. Do you have an aspirin? (BOY ONE hands her an aspirin and she pops it in her mouth.)

BOY ONE. Wasn't last night something? We had the place really rocking.

GIRL THREE. The whole town watched our show. I wonder if

we'll have that many at Munich tonight?

BOY THREE (as the bus driver, with a slight German accent). We are approaching now Dachau Concentration Camp.

GIRL THREE (looking out). Everything is so *green*.

BOY ONE. Like the Garden of Eden.

GIRL THREE. Even when it rains.

BOY ONE. It's so peaceful. The ground, a green blanket. And look at all the grapes. The vines are bursting.

GIRL THREE. Think how the prisoners, in World War Two, must have been fooled. They must have thought they were going someplace . . . safe.

BOY ONE. It's hard to believe this land held so much suffering . . . only forty years ago.

BOY THREE (as the bus driver, braking, as the OTHERS all lean forward). Dachau.

GIRL THREE. Look how the rain cleans the window when he stops.

BOY ONE. This is going to be interesting.

GIRL THREE (suddenly alarmed). Oh, no!

BOY ONE. What?

GIRL THREE. Those gates. (She refers to the two stepladders.) I've seen them before! (She shivers.) I'm so cold.

BOY ONE. But we haven't been in this part of Europe.

GIRL THREE (trying to compose herself). It's all right. I guess I was just experiencing deja vu. It's okay. I get this way once in a while. (She tries to shake her nervousness.) Look at that man's uniform: it looks as if the forest has spilled all over him.

BOY THREE. We drive now to main part of camp.

GIRL THREE (watching the gates recede, to herself). I feel as if I'm never going to leave.

GIRL FIVE (as the tour director, standing up beside BOY THREE). All right, boys and girls. Please stay together. Don't wander off from the group. If you take your camera, the management will not be responsible if it is lost. You will be divided into groups with a guide for each group. Lunch will be served after the tour of the concentration camp. Be back on time or you will be left behind. (ALL start to file off the bus.)

BOY ONE. Got your camera?

GIRL THREE. Don't want it.

BOY ONE. Your scarf? (GIRL THREE nods.)

GIRL THREE (to BOY THREE). See you later, Fritzie.

BOY THREE (as the bus driver). The name is Fritz.

GIRL THREE. I'm sorry. Aren't you coming?

BOY THREE (as the bus driver). No, sank you, fraulein. I don't like der place. Makes me nervous, but you have goot time.

GIRL THREE (shivering hard). Yeah, I know what you mean. I've got the creepy-crawlies already. (She steps off the bus.) Oh, no, right in a puddle!

BOY ONE (looking around). Looks like the camp's about as big as about a dozen football fields.

GIRL THREE. Look at all the rusty barbed wire. It almost seems to stick to the low clouds. (She puts her tongue out.) Mmmm, the raindrops taste good.

BOY ONE. That'll make you colder.

GIRL THREE. That's all right. It feels . . . clean. (She looks at BOY ONE and is startled.)

BOY ONE. What's the matter now?

GIRL THREE. Nothing, nothing.

BOY ONE. Yes, there is. What?

GIRL THREE. Oh . . . I don't know. I guess it's just the rain on your blond hair. For a second I saw you . . . oh, it's silly . . . I thought you were a Nazi soldier.

BOY ONE. You've been watching too many old movies. (He looks around and points.) Look, only one of the barracks is still standing. But you can see the foundations of the others.

GIRL THREE (non-commitally). Yeah.

BOY ONE. There's the gas chamber and crematorium. This was the second largest Jewish prison camp. Nearly a million and a half Jewish people were gassed in those two buildings.

GIRL THREE. It gives me the creeps.

BOY ONE. It doesn't bother me. (He pulls Girl Three's arm as they walk along.) This building is the shower or bath. Jewish people were first taken to the bath where they were gassed.

GIRL THREE (gasping slightly). How awful, to die in a gas chamber.

BOY ONE. And think of all the others who died from hunger, disease, beatings, and the so-called medical experiments. All because of Hitler's orders.

GIRL THREE. You're so matter-of-fact about it all.

BOY ONE (shrugging). The guide wants us to go into the office. (He and GIRL THREE move to another part of the stage.) Oh, it's a museum.

GIRL THREE. It smells like a cave. Like sulfur.

GIRL TWO (as the German guide). And zis, boys and girls, is an example already of the chiseled rocks from der granite hill. Dachau's motto was . . .

GIRL THREE (softly, to the audience, a split second before GIRL TWO). Arbet Macht Frei.

GIRL TWO (as the German guide, after a slight pause). Arbet Macht Frei, which meant Work Makes One Free.

GIRL THREE (bitterly). Arbet Macht Frei.

GIRL ONE (another student, nearby). What did you say?

GIRL THREE. Nothing.

GIRL ONE. Are you feeling okay, Sharon? You look tired today.

GIRL THREE. I'm fine. It's just . . . this place.

GIRL ONE. I know. It makes me sad.

GIRL THREE. Would you mind if I stayed by you for a while? I'm not feeling so great.

GIRL ONE. Sure. Come along.

GIRL THREE. Thanks. (The GROUP walks out of the office area.)

BOY ONE. Hey, here's the quarry where they did all the hard labor.

GIRL ONE. It's raining too hard. Let's go into the crematorium to get dry. (The GROUP walks into the crematorium area. ALL walk briskly except GIRL THREE, at the rear of the group, who stops at the entry and looks around wildly before slowly entering.)

GIRL TWO (as the German guide). And in concrete sculpture is der Zyklon-B crystals in glass.

BOY ONE. Wow! That's the prettiest thing here. What a lovely color of amethyst blue.

GIRL THREE (shuddering). Ugh.

GIRL TWO (as the German guide). And here is der shower room. Asphyxiation was a quick way of extermination. It took fifteen minutes only and was combined with incineration, all under one roof. The victims thought they were going through a delousing in a real shower. Very efficient. The gas escaped from the perforations in the sheet-metal columns up there. The victims were packed too tightly to notice and some would sit comfortably gazing up at the shower heads, from which no water came, or the floor which had no drainage holes. Then they would feel the gas and crowd away from the columns and stampede toward the huge metal door where they would pile up in one blue-faced, clammy, blood-spattered, naked pyramid.

GIRL FOUR. Please let me through! I've got to get out of here! (She leaves rapidly. BOY ONE helps her out. GIRL THREE shudders.)

GIRL TWO (as the German guide, droning on). After twenty minutes, electric pumps removed der poisonous air and the sonderkomandos wearing gas masks, gum boots, and carrying hoses went in to search for gold teeth and human hair. Then they put them in carts already to go to the furnaces. Follow me, please. (ALL wander along with GIRL TWO.)

GIRL THREE (leaving the group and joining BOY ONE and GIRL FOUR sitting by themselves). I can't bear to look at the ovens. May I join you?

BOY ONE. Sure. Sit down. (He offers her his seat.)

GIRL THREE. Thanks. (To GIRL FOUR.) How are you feeling now? I got worried about you.

GIRL FOUR. I'm okay. But I've been worried about *you* ever since we got here.

GIRL THREE. Well . . . it's strange, but I've been here before.

BOY ONE. Who-o.

GIRL THREE. Who-o yourself. I'm serious.

GIRL FOUR. Well, I'm totally spooked.

GIRL THREE. Is it almost time to go, I hope?

BOY ONE. Soon.

GIRL THREE (groaning). Oh, here they come again.

BOY ONE (taking Girl Three and Girl Four's hands). There's only one more stop — the barracks. Come on. There's nothing scary there.

GIRL FOUR. At least the rain has stopped. (GIRL THREE shivers uncontrollably.)

BOY ONE (putting his arm around GIRL THREE). Cold?

GIRL THREE (shrugging off Boy One's arm). Not that cold.

BOY ONE (quietly). It *is* cold. (He and the GIRLS walk.) Cellar Block Seven. Come on. (The two ladders form the doorway. GIRL THREE holds back. Suddenly, she impulsively grabs Boy One's hand and he leads her in.) Look. Nothing but wooden tables, chairs and beds. The beds are stacked five high. Wow.

GIRL TWO (as the German guide). You can picture der scene.

People sitting, chattering after the day's work was over. (GIRL THREE, still holding Boy One's hand, pulls back.)

BOY ONE. Sharon! What on earth is going on inside that head of yours?

GIRL THREE. All these doomed people keep staring at me. (To BOY ONE.) Sorry. Nothing.

BOY ONE. I may not be the world's greatest conversationalist, but I don't think I'm *that* boring.

GIRL TWO (as the German guide). In this part of the barracks, the young intelligentsia were kept. Many were used for medical experiments.

GIRL THREE (yanking her hand away from BOY ONE). I'm not going in that part of the room! (At this moment, the entire CAST reaches down quickly for bits and pieces of costume. Each of the BOYS puts on a Nazi swastika armband. The GIRLS grab gray, rag-like shawls and cover themselves. GIRL FOUR lies down and clutches her shawl, groaning piteously. GIRL THREE, horribly distraught, speaks with a slight German accent.) She's dying. I know she's dying. Oh, I itch so badly. There's nothing in my stomach. No privacy, ever. People are dying every hour. Just now a lady gave birth to a stillborn baby. My eight-year-old son died four months ago. I can't work anymore. I'm too tired all the time. Mary Shapiro, who was here three months, was shot because she said she had a dream that God told her we'd be delivered from our misery by spring. Oh, I pray that's true. If I could only hold out 'til then.

BOY ONE (as the BOYS rush into the barracks, holding imaginary machine guns). Everyvun, line up against der wall! Pull dat fraulein out of her bed! (BOY THREE yanks GIRL FOUR from her bed and shoves her with the OTHERS. GIRL THREE is slightly apart from the other GIRLS. GIRL FOUR slumps to the floor. BOY THREE hauls her upright again.) Now! Fire!

(All the BOYS fire their machine guns. If possible, terrifying-
ly-loud noises over the sound system would be ideal; imaginary
guns would give a more powerful effect. The GIRLS writhe
and fall dead.)

GIRL THREE. Ohhhh! The blood! The blood! It's running
through the cracks in the floor!

BOY ONE (approaching GIRL THREE). And you! (He stalks
her slowly, then pulls an imaginary pistol from his holster.
GIRL THREE cowers. He places the gun at the side of her
head and fires. GIRL THREE slumps to the floor. After a
slight pause, the BOYS walk out. Quietly, ALL take off the
armbands and shawls and become American students again.
ALL leave the barracks. To GIRL THREE.) Sharon? Sharon,
are you okay?

GIRL THREE (rubbing her head where the gunshot had been).
I . . . guess so. I've got a terrible headache . . . right here.
(BOY ONE gently escorts her to a seat.)

BOY ONE. Better?

GIRL THREE. I feel . . . exhausted . . . as if I had just sprint-
ed a whole mile. (A pause.) It was . . . that very . . . room.
(She pauses, then suddenly begins to cry.)

BOY ONE. Hey, it's okay. You just sit there and catch your
breath. (He puts his arm around GIRL THREE.)

GIRL THREE. Thanks. Let's go back on the bus. (ALL put
the bus back together and get on. GIRL THREE is next to
last.) Wait.

BOY ONE. What?

GIRL THREE. I need . . . to take . . . one more look. (She
looks.) I wanted to see . . . the barracks one more time . . .
but, funny, all I can see is . . . your profile . . . still looking
like a young soldier. Oh, well. (She gets on the bus, followed
by BOY ONE. They sit in their seats and she looks out the
window, slowly turning her head backward, staring, as the bus

departs. After a pause, there is a brief musical bridge.)
BOY THREE. Talk about a powerful story!
GIRL FOUR. I *know*. For a change, let's do something romantic. (The OTHERS scoff.)
BOY ONE. I've got it. We'll each do our very favorite short poem. Really short.
GIRL ONE. Okay. (She speaks thoughtfully, slowly.)
    This journey inside myself . . .
    like crossing a river.
    It is cold . . .
    and the current is strong.
BOY ONE (seriously, very close to GIRL ONE).
    You are like a blue lake.
    Just when I feel I can see to the bottom,
    I discover unknown depths.
GIRL TWO (looking up, enjoying the sensuous warmth).
    Summer sunshine high,
    Playing with fire,
    Shooting to heaven,
    Bleeds orange warmth on me.
BOY TWO (pantomiming with so much pleasure that ALL can feel it).
    It's so nice to feel
    the icy smooth wood of my fiddle,
    warming up,
    under my chin.
GIRL THREE (sadly picking a flower).
    The daffodil has
    gone. Why do the leaves look so
    suddenly hostile?
GIRL FOUR (romantically).
    Rainstorm

Crashes on the
Roof, making thunder in
The attic and rainbows across
My heart.
BOY THREE (using his arms vigorously).
"The dining room centerpiece."
Twisted and fractured,
The drift wood
Standing upon its base
Directed the meal
With its splintered arms.
GIRL FIVE (enjoying the sounds).
Spring
was
sky-blue.
Windex,
squeaking
against
kitchen
window panes.
GIRL ONE. That was great. Let's go 'round again and make
'em even better! (She becomes aware of Boy One's sultry
stare.)
This summer the days do not fly
by on tanned wings.
But plunge like hot molten lead
into the cool water of my life.
BOY ONE (embracing GIRL ONE but looking over her
shoulder at the audience).
She kisses you,
eyes closed.
You feel passion
and love.
And . . .

GIRL ONE.
>   She feels guilty
>   because
>   she's thinking about
>   someone else.

GIRL TWO (with loving warmth).
>   The old woman
>   picked the flowers
>   as if they were
>   her children.

GIRL THREE.
>   Hate is red,
>   it sounds like thunder,
>   it smells like spoiled milk,
>   it tastes like a rotten lemon,
>   and feels like cold rain.
> (She twists away.)

BOY TWO (as squishy-sticky as he can make the sounds, enjoying
   himself).
>   "Mud."
>   Squishing through ten toes . . .
>   Nose knowing no fragrant rose . . .
>   Prose cannot describe . . . mud.

GIRL FOUR (with great love).
>   My grandmother is
>   a little hand-knitted sweater
>   of yarned memories,
>   and a china tea cup
>   without a handle.

BOY THREE (clowning and pantomiming with great excitement).
>   The dark condemns me to the
>   middle of my bed,

no foot hanging over for the
alligator to grab.
GIRL FIVE (with great delight).
The sky is tall, towering, glowering today.
The whole dome is painted a hot water-color blue.
(She points in mock accusation.)
And *you* , a tiny round wisp of white,
Have the delicious audacity to be
The only cloud in *my* sky.
(ALL laugh.)
GIRL ONE. That was great. What a bunch of *vivid* poems.
BOY THREE. You wanna hear *vivid*? Here's vivid. It's my
favorite great literature.
GIRL ONE. I bet.
BOY THREE. It's called "Hateful Things." But you guys all
gotta help. (ALL cluster around, giggling and ad-libbing
remarks such as "Okay, here we go!")
Moldy cheese and boiled beets,
Book reports and smelly feets.
GIRL FIVE.
Politicians, sauerkraut,
Boxers who can't win one bout.
GIRL ONE.
Smoking, drinking, plastic swords,
Fingernails on the boards.
BOY ONE.
Texans, okra, pink and punk,
Rotten fruit and mushy junk.
GIRL TWO.
Eggplant, colds and gum on shoes,
Fuzzy dice and tabloid news.

BOY TWO.
AC/DC "Back in black,"
Itches in your upper back.
GIRL THREE.
Tests and peas and Valley Girls,
Homework, tofu, phony pearls.
GIRL FOUR.
Andy Griffith, carrot juice,
Discos, BeeGees, marmalade . . .
ALL. And Mother Goose! (ALL laugh enthusiastically.)
GIRL THREE (enjoying her first real relaxation of the evening).
Hey, that was fun. (ALL agree loudly.)
BOY THREE. And I've got something ten times funnier than *that*. It's a story called "The Goddess in Tennis Shoes."
GIRL FIVE. Great. Let's hear it.
BOY THREE. All right. And you play the goddess.
GIRL FIVE. A goddess? You've gotta be kidding.
BOY THREE. I'm not. Ready? Here we go! (ALL form a classroom and sit.) My mind wandered free from the purply ditto sheet that glared at me.
GIRL ONE (as the teacher). Now, class, you must concentrate on your spelling test.
BOY THREE. While my fourth grade classmates labored like vassals in medieval England, I ventured fearlessly into the dim hallways of a Gothic castle. (He gets up, his eyes focused far away, and wanders downstage.) I knew the odds I had to face.
GIRL FOUR (from her seat, a voice in his imagination). Sir Butch, Warwick Castle is manned by five hundred guards. (The stepladders may be battlements.)
GIRL TWO (from her seat, another voice in his imagination). And their lances are tipped with poison.
BOY THREE (in highly-inflated language). Deep within me surged a raw courage that no other member of the human race

had ever experienced. My blood boiled and froth bubbled at the corners of my lips. (He slobbers.) Stealthily, I slid my sword from its scabbard and with an intense fury, I charged into the very jaws of death! (The sword is imaginary. The OTHERS quietly get up from their schoolroom and, in glassy-eyed slow motion, begin to surround BOY THREE and pantomime their sword-and-shield warfare.) *Millions* of guards pressed upon me. They oozed in from battlements and secret passageways. Wave upon wave of arrows rained on my shield, but I battled onward. With the strength of a score of men, I methodically slashed down the demented fiends. (As he "kills" each attacker, the ATTACKER gargles or screams or groans, spins and spirals in slow motion, gradually moving silently in slow motion back into the classroom seat held before.) Finally, the brutal conflict was o'er. All was silent. With wild anticipation in my throbbing chest, I lunged toward the oaken door behind which lay the treasure for which I had risked my life. (He lurches toward his seat.) I reached out a trembling hand and threw it open. There, sitting with her back to me, was the most beautiful maiden in all the world. She was my goddess. (He refers to GIRL FIVE, seated directly in front of him. He slides back into his seat and his voice for the following line is totally different from his previously inflated reverie. He is flatly matter-of-fact.) She was taking a spelling test.

GIRL ONE (as the teacher). Butch, are you concentrating on your test?

BOY THREE (ignoring GIRL ONE). My desk was directly behind hers, but miles of space lay between us. She was a goddess and I merely an underpaid defender of freedom and righteousness. (He sighs.) I struggled to spell some insignificant word. Its meaning I knew not. Was "i" before "e" except after

"c," or "x" before "q" except after "k?" I left that one blank.
GIRL ONE (as the teacher). Butch, are you finished?
BOY THREE. Yes, Miss McNoodle. (He takes his test to GIRL ONE, then stares longingly at GIRL FIVE from very close range as he walks up and back. GIRL FIVE ignores him.)
GIRL ONE (as the teacher). Sit down and remain quiet.
BOY THREE. What a vision! I loved everything about her! I loved her wonderful, medieval, romantic name: Patty! I loved her hair that hung near the front of my desk. (He twists Girl Five's hair. GIRL FIVE reaches back and slaps him fiercely.)
GIRL FIVE. Cut that out!
BOY THREE. I loved her dulcet voice. I even loved her ears! Her ears had style and grace. (GIRL FIVE chews her pencil.) And she had a way of chewing her number two lead pencil that drove me wild. (He cranes his neck to look over Girl Five's shoulder.) She never left teeth marks!
GIRL ONE (as the teacher). Butch, sit still!
BOY THREE. But what impressed me most was her attire. While the others wore little-girl sandals or slip-ons, Patty wore the most fantastic black tennis shoes I'd ever beheld. They were daringly low-cut and had red stripes down the sides! (He bends way down to look at Girl Five's shoes, then sits back up in his desk.) *What a woman*! (BOY ONE makes a loud, ding-a-ling sound for the school bell. ALL push and shove out of the classroom, leaving BOY THREE to bring up the rear.) Now came time for my long and perilous journey home. (He walks bizarrely slow). I kept my hands on the hilt of my trusty sword, sensing that dangers lay ahead. Thrice that week had I been ambushed by marauding highwaymen. But thrice I had beaten them back and emerged triumphant without even a smudge on my gleaming armor.
GIRL FIVE (quietly). Hey, cut that out.
BOY THREE. Hark! What do I hear?
GIRL FIVE (louder, as BOY ONE teases her). Stop it, John!

BOY THREE. It's Patty! (He runs and discovers BOY ONE chasing GIRL FIVE. Both are acting like small school children.)

GIRL FIVE. I'm gonna tell my mama!

BOY THREE. It was Moose Kroobing, the local sixth-grade bully. (BOY ONE stands tall. BOY THREE stands very short. For a moment, they are nose to nose, with BOY ONE towering.) Heroes never worry about size. Immediately I seized my blade and wielded it above my head, ready to strike. (He swings his imaginary sword.)

GIRL FIVE (running by and hitting BOY ONE teasingly). Don't you dare, Moose!

BOY THREE. Take that! (He gingerly sticks out a foot as BOY ONE starts to chase GIRL FIVE. BOY ONE stumbles, comes to a stop and wheels toward BOY THREE. He towers over the crouching BOY THREE.)

BOY ONE. Arrrrrggghhh!

BOY THREE (in a very small voice). W-what?

BOY ONE (with a loud snarl). You wanna fight?

BOY THREE (gulping, swallowing, cowering). N-no.

BOY ONE (grunting). Good. (He runs after GIRL FIVE, who is happily waiting at the far side of the stage. They walk off together.)

BOY THREE (gradually coming from his bent-over position to a very erect posture and speaking in the inflated tone again). I stared through the visor of my helmet as the monster disappeared into the mists of Cawdor. (He starts to swagger.) Then . . . miraculously . . . my sword reappeared out of the air. (He reaches up for it, pauses, smiles cockily, then speaks in a normal voice.) That was fortunate because I had to slay a dragon and rescue a toad from an evil wizard on my way home. (He dances away.)

GIRL THREE (after a pause, to BOY THREE and GIRL FIVE, in a quiet, walls-down but friendly moment). Even when you're acting out a story, you still hide from things, don't you?

BOY THREE (sheepishly). I guess . . . sometimes.

GIRL FIVE. So what if we do? (After a slight pause, friendly.) But you let everything get to you. Is that any better?

GIRL THREE (sheepishly). Probably not.

GIRL FOUR. I know what you mean. I act romantic and all, but I do know there's a rough world out there.

GIRL TWO. But one that's worth living in.

BOY TWO. Amen!

BOY ONE. What say we close with some poems that express our feelings right now?

GIRL ONE. Good idea. You start.

BOY ONE (facing GIRL ONE).

   "I love you."
  Not as dramatic as before,
  But meaning just as much,
  And more.
  I was prepared for no answer.
  You can live with it
  (I told myself.)
  But you answered me . . .
 (He smiles.)
  With your eyes,
  And your surprise.

GIRL ONE (to BOY ONE as they walk very slowly, intent upon each other).

  Let's walk softly and whisper,
  And just smile at one another.
  Let's not even talk very much,
  And let's touch gently at first.
  Glass shatters, and we might break.

GIRL THREE (finally without any anger at all).
   When I was a little girl
   Climbing stairs and chasing calico cats,
   There was a cedar chest,
   And I would go treasure hunting.
   There were scrapbooks and letters and birthday cards.
   There were old pictures of young couples
   With soft skin and frozen faces.
   There was a love letter from the cowboy
   That Mother married. It was funny.
  (A pause.)
   I found the secret of life when I was six years old.
  (A pause.)
   My mother had saved it.
GIRL FOUR (with a quick, smiling embrace of GIRL THREE).
   That's *nice*. (GIRL THREE grins.) Feeling better now?
GIRL THREE. Yes. (ALL smile warmly and give her positive
   non-verbals.)

GIRL 4 (Radiantly.)
Sunlight on the bay,
Starlight in the sky,
And tinsel in the sea at midnight.
Fingers in the cheesecake,
Fingers in the wax,
And fingers connecting hands to hands.
Endless days and endless questions with silly answers,
And a bunch of crazy kids fooling around.
Sunlight on the bay,
Starlight in the sky,
And tinsel in the sea at midnight.
Shining eyes and dancing hearts
And laughter . . . always laughter ringing across the open sea.
GIRL TWO. Here's one for all of us to do together. (Each reflects his or her character and acts out the appropriate actions.)
Adolescence is . . .
GIRL THREE. A balloon in a room full of pins.
BOY TWO. A five-thousand piece puzzle.
GIRL FOUR. That rain in March.
BOY THREE. A clown in the circus!
GIRL FIVE. A three-D monster movie.
BOY ONE. A kite flying on a gusty day.

BOY THREE. A messy room.

GIRL ONE. A pair of ballet slippers thrown in the bottom of a closet.

GIRL FOUR. A fresh patch of red raspberries.

GIRL FIVE. A weed.

GIRL THREE. A brick wall.

BOY TWO. A bubble . . . ready to burst!

BOY ONE. A spider spinning off into the wind.

GIRL TWO. A pimple.

GIRL ONE. And . . . a rainbow filled with music. (ALL smile, appreciating each other's efforts.)

BOY THREE (to GIRL FIVE, as they grinningly lean against each other, back to back, at a steep angle).
You're always there
even when I'm not,
And you're always comforting
so I can feel safe.
Leanable,
Liveable,
And warm
are the words for you.
They fit.
And I love you . . .
(Surprised at the phrase, BOTH jerk their heads to look at each other.)
As much as I love
any . . .
(A pause.)
sofa pillow!
(He giggles. GIRL FIVE swats him as he leans away.)

GIRL FIVE. Someone asked me the other day,

BOY THREE. "What Do You Want?"

GIRL FIVE.
 I merely said, "A Pepsi, please."
 But I lied.
 What I want
 is to be out on my own
 with a good job
 and dinner that tastes better
 than the pan it was cooked in.
 What I want
 is an "A" grade-point average,
 but not to study 'til midnight
 to get it.
 What I want
 is a life with no children
 tugging and pulling
 until my arms drag on the ground.
 But for now . . .
 (A pause.)
 I'll take a Pepsi.
(She acts as if she might kiss BOY THREE, then jumps back, grinning.)
BOY ONE (to BOY THREE and GIRL FIVE). All right, you guys, come on.
BOY THREE (too innocently). What?
GIRL ONE (joining in). You *know* what. All night long you guys have been horsing around, afraid of your real feelings.
GIRL FIVE. Who, me?
BOY ONE. Yes! Come on!
BOY THREE. Well . . .
GIRL FIVE. Well . . . (BOY ONE takes Girl Five's hand. GIRL ONE takes Boy Three's hand. They join together and step back. The OTHERS cheer.)

BOY THREE (embarrassed, to GIRL FIVE). I guess you're . . .
all right.
GIRL FIVE (with a warm grin). Thanks. (A slight pause.) But
don't pick on *us*. These guys have been afraid to *speak* to each
other all night. (She indicates BOY TWO and GIRL TWO.
The OTHERS loudly agree.)
BOY ONE. Come on!
GIRL ONE. No holding back! (BOY TWO gets his courage up.
He goes to GIRL TWO, takes her by the hand and leads her
forward from the group which remains assembled behind them.
They finally allow themselves to look at each other with
radiance. Their voices are quiet but filled with deep affection.)
GIRL TWO.
You gave me a frozen rose bud
wrapped in snow.
BOY TWO.
I said it was our love preserved
and you were to unwrap it
when it was ready to bloom.
Remember how you buried
your cold little hands
in the warm, dry leaves
scattered on the sleepy sidewalk?
GIRL TWO.
You tossed me up and watched
white winds brush my hair.
We rolled in laughter
and stared in amazement
into a mirror of
stone and water
with silent motions of a faded summer,
reflecting into a gentle picture of winter.

BOY TWO.
Quiet laughter was the
background.
I saved a winter . . . just for you.
(He holds hands with GIRL TWO. There is great affection as
each reaches outward and ALL come forward and hold hands
for a curtain call. There is a final chord or two, or appropriate
music.)

CURTAIN

THE STAGE:

An empty stage with two stepladders, some chairs, cubes or small platforms, or a combination of all three, to create ever-changing angles and elevations. Make the pieces light, portable and simple.

Try to find appropriate stage action for as much as possible throughout the script.

THE PLAYERS:

The cast members should be dressed as simply as possible to facilitate easy movement about the stage.

The Student Writers, Their Schools and Teachers
In Order of Presentation

Erica Moss
Highland High, Albuquerque
Teacher: Libby Russell
Lea Daugherty
Lovington High School
Teacher: Virginia Rogers
Emily Nye
Santa Fe Preparatory School
Teacher: Robert Saam
Sherry Vanderwalker
Mountain View High, Mesa
Teacher: Richard Saggio
Kathi Parker
Eldorado High, Albuquerque
Teacher: Elizabeth Sleeter
Jane McIntyre
Highland High, Albuquerque
Teacher: Fred Hayes
Rachael Hernandez
Riverside High, El Paso
Teacher: Honie Lou Laster
R. Elizabeth Arbiter
Santa Rita High, Tucson
Teacher: Roger Shanley
Leslie Bennick
Manzano High, Albuquerque
Teacher: Alan Stringer
Patricia Sallen
Casa Grande High School
Teacher: Barbara Warren

Kristin Rasciner
Sunnyslope High, Phoenix
Teacher: Terri Fields
Valerie Ingram
Santa Fe High School
Teacher: Mary Rita Haufman
Ruben Ramirez
Sahuaro High, Tucson
Teacher: Rita Garitano
Marta Murvosh
Valley High, Las Vegas
Teacher: Robert Salchert
Betsy Peticolas
Coronado High, El Paso
Teacher: Sulta Yates
Katie Kramer
Santa Fe Preparatory School
Teacher: Robert Saam
Frank Messina
Manzano High, Albuquerque
Teacher: Alan Stringer
Jared Hamilton
Silver City High School
Teacher: Dianne Orwig
Sylvia Aldaz
Ysleta High, El Paso
Teacher: Juawanna Newman
Diann Spendlove
Dixie High, St. George
Teacher: Karen Lopez
Judy Ryan
Manzano High, Albuquerque
Teacher: Alan Stringer
Nadine Montoya
Espanola Valley High School
Teacher: Jim Sagel

Lenny Wallis
Washington High, Phoenix
Teacher: Don Engelbrecht
Tracie Hunteman
Eldorado High, Albuquerque
Teacher: Elizabeth Sleeter
David Streater
Highland High, Albuquerque
Teacher: Fred Hayes
Judy Ryan
Manzano High, Albuquerque
Teacher: Alan Stringer
Anita Ingro
Manzano High, Albuquerque
Teacher: Alan Stringer
Joseph H. McCoy
Las Cruces High School
Teacher: Phyllis Wright
Sue Robbins
Highland High, Albuquerque
Teacher: Fred Hayes
Bonnie Zoller
Espanola Valley High School
Teacher: Catherine Mayer
Judy Ryan
Manzano High, Albuquerque
Teacher: Alan Stringer
Ted Cote
Mountain View High, Mesa
Teacher: Richard Saggio
William F. Murphy
Mesa High School
Teacher: Billie Cox

Philip H. Mahoney
Manzano High, Albuquerque
Teacher: Alan Stringer
*Karla Baca**
Manzano High, Albuquerque
Teacher: Alan Stringer
Paula McIntosh
Santa Fe High School
Teacher: Beverly McCrary-LeMunyon
Grace Tredwell
Santa Fe Preparatory School
Teacher: Robert Saam
Miguel Martinez
East High, Phoenix
Teacher: Cheryl Byers
Margaret Cooper Field
Santa Fe Preparatory School
Teacher: Robert Saam
Larry Warner
Moon Valley High, Phoenix
Teacher: Carolyn Ann Sheley
Louise Waller
Rincon High, Tucson
Teacher: Jean Christison
Michael Downs
Santa Rita High, Tucson
Dawn Maxwell
Manzano High, Albuquerque
Teacher: Alan Stringer
Walter McConnell
Manzano High, Albuquerque
Teacher: Alan Stringer

Elizabeth Green
Mountain View High, Mesa
Teacher: Richard Saggio
Suzy Hahn
Las Cruces High School
Teacher: Phyllis Wright
Karen Baca
Santa Fe High School
Robin Rever
Santa Rita High, Tucson
Teacher: Roger Shanley
Tim Bajema
Santa Fe High School
Teacher: Ben Rael
Jill Benoist
Santa Fe Preparatory School
Teacher: Robert Saam
Paul Fox
Highland High, Albuquerque
Teacher: Fred Hayes
Kelly Rae
Washington High, Phoenix
Teacher: Don Engelbrecht
Kellie Sharon
Mountain View High, Mesa
Teacher: Richard Saggio
Sharon Zotigh
Manzano High, Albuquerque
Teacher: Alan Stringer
Hal McDuffie
Santa Fe High School
Teacher: Beverly McCrary-LeMunyon
Karol Larsen
Manzano High, Albuquerque
Teacher: Alan Stringer

Rebecca Flanick
Moon Valley High, Phoenix
Teacher: Carolyn Ann Sheley
Kathleen Brennan
Highland High, Albuquerque
Teacher: Fred Hayes
Betsy Cunningham
Highland High, Albuquerque
Teacher: Shirley Smith
Theresa Marleau
Deming High School
Teacher: Harvielee Offutt Moore
Susan Watt
Los Alamos High School
Teacher: Jeanne Lawton
Laurie Bacastow
Los Alamos High School
Teacher: Jeanne Lawton
Traude Crosswhite
Mayfield High, Las Cruces
Teacher: Warren Cupp
Stephanie Lupenski
Highland High, Albuquerque
Teacher: Fred Hayes
Kitty Riordan
Highland High, Albuquerque
Teacher: Fred Hayes
Joe Chavez
Laguna-Acoma High School
Teacher: Dorothy O'Neal
Scott Gerber
Santa Fe Preparatory School
Teacher: Irene Epp

Patsy Packard
Sandia High, Albuquerque
Teacher: Muriel Beaven
David Van Antwerp
Manzano High, Albuquerque
Teacher: Alan Stringer
Jill Benoist
Santa Fe Preparatory School
Teacher: Robert Saam
Jay F. Turley
Santa Fe High School
Teacher: Beverly McCrary-LeMunyon
Martin English
Westwood High, Mesa
Teacher: Joyce Huffaker
Jessi L. Penniman
Sandia Preparatory School, Albuquerque
Teacher: William Woodard
Katie Kramer
Santa Fe Preparatory School
Teacher: Robert Saam
Molly Beasley
Alamogordo High School
Teacher: Faye Lee
Linda Kinney
Rincon High, Tucson
Teacher: Freeman B. Hover
Hillary Paskiewicz
Santa Fe High School
Teacher: Nancy Armbruster
Karen Gregory
Highland High, Albuquerque
Teacher: Fred Hayes

Dawn Maxwell
Manzano High, Albuquerque
Teacher: Alan Stringer

** Karla Baca's poem supplied the title for this show.*

NOTES